Late Shift

The death of retirement

Late Shift

The death of retirement

Richard Tomlinson

POLITICO'S

First published in Great Britain 2007 by
Politico's Publishing, an imprint of
Methuen Publishing Ltd
11–12 Buckingham Gate
London
SW1E 6LB

1

A CIP catalogue record for this book is available from the British Library.

ISBN 978-1-84275-203-6

Typeset in Garamond by SX Composing DTP, Rayleigh, Essex
Printed and bound in Great Britain by MPG Books, Bodmin, Cornwall

Contents

To my daughter
Hannah

Note about names

The research for this book was organised around 130 interviews with people in the Reading area. Most of the interviewees were happy to be identified, but in a few cases they preferred to remain anonymous. I have also decided not to identify four people who said I could use their names, because some of their comments seemed personally or professionally sensitive.

I have therefore adopted the following style rules when naming people: the name is real where both a first name and a surname are used, for example Anne Murch; the name is invented where only a first name is used, for example Don.

Note about chronology

All the interviews for the main body of the book were conducted between May 2005 and May 2006. In September 2006, I recontacted nearly all the interviewees (a few proved impossible to trace) to discover how they had fared in the meantime. These later interviews are recorded in the Epilogue.

Readers who wish to find out the most recent news about an interviewee should therefore consult the Epilogue, where people appear in order of their place in the narrative.

1   The late life crisis

Four builders have just downed tools for their mid-morning break at Purley Magna, a derelict eighteenth-century Berkshire mansion that is being converted into luxury apartments. Over tea in the site manager's hut, Dave King, John Cochrane, Brian Strange and Dave Hicks complain about poor pay and long hours like builders everywhere. But these four friends are unusual for their trade in one respect. Three of them are in their sixties, while Dave Hicks is seventy-three. John reckons they are more than twice the average age of the rest of the workforce on this building site.

So why are they still working in a tough, strenuous industry, when the majority of their age group have already retired?

'For the money, really,' says Brian, a laconic 64-year-old carpenter who is saving up to emigrate to Spain.

Money – or the lack of it – is the main reason that has brought all of them to Purley Magna, three miles west of Reading. Dave King, a 63-year-old bricklayer, is also planning to emigrate, and needs cash to finance a reconnaissance trip to Australia with his wife, sister and brother-in-law. John, 62, is writing a historical novel set in ancient Rome during the reign of the emperor Nero. 'But I've got to be realistic. I can't see it being a huge bestseller as far as sales are concerned.' Meanwhile, Dave Hicks is repairing his finances after the small building firm that he used to run went out of business.

As they finish their tea, the four insist that they are all fit enough to carry on working. Indeed, these Reading builders are in the vanguard of a movement that could transform the workplace over the coming decades, for two compelling reasons. First, a combination of low birth rates and rising life expectancy will radically alter the age structure of societies throughout the developed world. Some countries, such as Japan and Italy, face an especially daunting demographic transition. But the populations of all countries in the Organisation for Economic Co-operation and Development (OECD), including Britain, will age dramatically (see Figure 1.1).

Figure 1.1: Percentage of population aged 65 and over in OECD countries 2000–2050

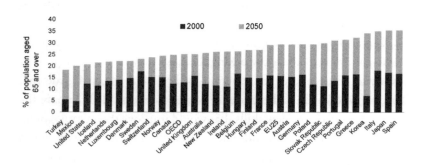

Based on Fig. 1.1 in *Ageing and Employment Policies: Live Longer, Work Longer*, p. 18, © OECD 2006.

The four builders are lucky. They work in an industry where there is high demand for skilled, experienced craftsmen whose long career in the trade is actually an advantage, provided they are physically fit and in good health. A growing number of people over the age of fifty in Britain, as elsewhere in the developed world, are far less fortunate. They want to continue working through their sixties and perhaps into their seventies, either full time or part time, because they like their jobs or are worried about financing their retirement – or both. But they work for employers who are still wedded to a culture in which capable and productive older people are expected to retire without complaint by their mid-sixties, to create vacancies for younger staff.

It is true that Britain's first age discrimination law, passed in October 2006, has defined the legal limits of this hidebound employment culture. Under the law, employers cannot force employees to retire purely because of their age until they are sixty-five. The government has promised to review this clause in the law in 2011, when most campaigners for older workers' rights expect it will be scrapped.

It is also true that there are many people in the fifty-plus age group who cannot wait to stop working, because they dislike their jobs or want to enjoy a long retirement – or both. Finally, it is true that people who have a bad experience of work are least likely to have the willingness to learn new skills that would improve their employment prospects in their fifties and sixties – thus reinforcing the widespread stereotype of older people as slower, less adaptable, and therefore less employable in a rapidly changing economy.

Yet despite these caveats, two facts are clear from the testimony of Dave Hicks and his friends, and from well over 100 other people in the fifty-plus age group in one English town who were interviewed for this book. First, Britain's imperfect age discrimination law is merely an attempt to catch up with a change in the demographic composition of the workforce – not just in Britain, but throughout the developed world – that promises to be as significant as the end of child labour in the nineteenth century. Second, if present demographic trends continue, the ageing of the workforce will soon make a mockery of the idea that anyone should be forced to retire simply because they have reached their sixty-fifth birthday.

Already, this steady ageing process has altered the traditional balance in a person's life between work and retirement. In 1950, a British man ending his career at the average retirement age of 67.2 years had a life expectancy of just 10.8 years, but by 2005, the same typical man could expect to live for a further 20.4 years after retirement at an average age of 64.0 years. In the same period, the life expectancy at retirement for the average British woman rose from 16.2 years to 25.1 years (see Table 1.1).

Table 1.1: Percentage of adult life spent in retirement in Britain

	Average age of exit from workforce	Life expectancy at age of exit from workforce	Percentage of adult life spent in retirement
1950 men	67.2	10.8	18.0%
women	63.9	16.2	26.1%
1960 men	66.2	11.5	19.3%
women	62.7	18.1	28.8%
1970 men	65.4	12.5	20.9%
women	62.4	19.4	30.4%
1980 men	64.6	14.3	23.5%
women	62.0	20.6	31.9%
1990 men	63.5	17.2	27.4%
women	60.9	23.2	35.1%
1995 men	63.1	18.9	29.5%
women	60.7	24.7	36.6%
2000 men	63.3	20.2	30.8%
women	61.1	25.2	36.9%
2005 men	64.0	20.4	30.7%
women	61.9	25.1	36.4%

Source: *A New Pensions Settlement for the Twenty-First Century: Second Report of the Pensions Commission* (London: Pensions Commission, 2005), p. 97.

This upward trend is set to continue. Between 2005 and 2050 the ratio of British people over sixty-five compared with those in the 20–64 age group is predicted to rise from 27 per cent to 47 per cent.* During the same period, the average life expectancy of a British man retiring at sixty-five is expected to increase from twenty to twenty-four years, while a British woman retiring at sixty will see her life expectancy rise from twenty-two years to twenty-six.[†]

These demographic trends are radically altering attitudes to retirement. Millions of people in their forties and fifties are waking up to the fact that their pension provision is inadequate, particularly as many of them will live into their eighties or older. They will have to save more and work longer to have any chance of a financially secure retirement. Even then, their old age may be overshadowed by money worries, because the government's promised long-term overhaul of Britain's creaking pension system will arrive too late to benefit many of those already in the fifty-plus age group.

The starting point for this overhaul is the second report of the government-appointed Pension Commission, led by Lord Turner, who presented his recommendations in November 2005. Turner called for a gradual rise in the state pension age to sixty-eight by 2050 for both men and women; reform of Britain's convoluted state pension system to make it easier to understand and less means tested; and the establishment of a cost-efficient National Pensions Savings Scheme, funded by both employers and employees, in which everyone would be automatically enrolled (with the right to opt out).

The government and the main opposition parties have broadly accepted most of Turner's recommendations, despite initial objections by the Treasury about restoring the link between the basic

---

A New Pensions Settlement for the Twenty-First Century: Second Report of the Pensions Commission (London: Pensions Commission, 2005), p. 94.
[†]Ibid., p. 89.

state pension and rises in average earnings. Labour is now formally committed to reinstating the link by 2012, 'subject to affordability'. While that sounds like a get-out clause, Turner is pleased that the politicians are finally unscrambling Britain's pension mess:

> I think the unique feature of Britain is the sheer complexity of the system we've produced . . . We've ended up with a basic state pension that is not enough to keep people out of poverty, and a whole layer of means-tested stuff on top of that, and an earnings-related pension system which is pretty inadequate in total and which has got salami sliced so many times to bring it back within the budgetary constraint that nobody can understand what they are entitled to.

Thus Turner has provided a framework for the debate about how Britain can afford an ageing society. Yet pension reform is not the whole story, especially since the proposed changes will not take effect in time to help many people in late middle age with insufficient retirement savings. For Britain to cope with this demographic revolution, employers will have to abandon the traditional concept of a 'natural' career span that ends somewhere between sixty and sixty-five. In the future, there will be more older workers like Dave Hicks and his friends who will need to extend their careers for financial reasons. Many older people will also want to continue in either full-time or part-time employment because they do not feel ready to retire. 'We like work,' says Dave simply, as he puts on his hard hat and heads back with his colleagues to the building site.

But can corporate Britain adapt to this late shift? The prospects for a smooth transition to the new, greyer world of work are not encouraging, despite the introduction in October 2006 of Britain's first age discrimination law. Under the law, companies cannot impose mandatory retirement on employees before they are sixty-five, and have to consider seriously any request to continue working beyond that age. Yet this clause – which, as already noted, will be reviewed in 2011 – actually represents a climbdown by the government, after the Confederation of British Industry (CBI) successfully lobbied against the removal of any upper age limit for forcible retirement. In a bizarre twist, the CBI's position was supported by the Trades Union Congress, on the grounds that without a universal default retirement age, employees would risk being required to work longer in order to claim company pensions. The absurd outcome is that the new age discrimination law is itself inherently ageist.

Del Wardle, a quietly determined account executive at Cox & Wyman, a printing firm in Reading, confirms from his own experience how even a relatively enlightened employer can remain wedded to the traditional management view of a natural career span. Del's problem was that he did not want to stop working in August 2006, when he reached the company's default retirement age of sixty-five. He explains his motives in Cox & Wyman's meeting room, beside an old photo album filled with pictures of veteran employees in the 1950s and 1960s receiving retirement presents from the managing director on their sixty-fifth birthday.

Del's wife died in 2004, and with both of his sons now grown up and married, office life has become his main solace. He says: 'I used to look into the future and think my wife was still going to be there, and it would be nice to be together and do all those things like travel. To have these people [at Cox & Wyman] around me actually made a great difference.' Del also recoils at the idea of spending all his time with people his age: 'I'm in a maisonette, and most of the people in the block are, let's say, retired ladies. One of the women said, "I've got your name down for our club, because there's a waiting list." And I thought, "Well, I'm not ready for that."'

But Del does not see himself as a charity case for Cox & Wyman.

He thinks the company would benefit from keeping him on: 'There is the experience thing . . . The principal customer I've been dealing with for a long time now doesn't want a change. If your brain's still active, and you're physically active, I think you can go on in customer service.'

For over a year, Del patiently lobbied to be allowed to continue full time at Cox & Wyman without making any headway. In the summer of 2006 he at last began to break down the management's resistance. Cox & Wyman initially said that he would have to stop working on his sixty-fifth birthday, but that after a break, he could start again on a short-term contract. Three weeks before the deadline, he was informed that he could simply carry on as normal. He recalls: 'It was rather strange on the first day after my birthday. I sat on the bus coming into work and I thought, "I don't need to do this."'

Del was fortunate in having an employer who was (in the end) sympathetic to his cause. Yet this is not the norm, says Patrick Grattan, chief executive of The Age and Employment Network, a campaigning group for older people in the workplace. Grattan argues that many companies still have 'antediluvian' attitudes towards employees over fifty: 'The perception that older workers are stale, less productive, ill more often and cost more is still extremely widespread.'

This mindset can be found even in companies that pride themselves on their anti-ageist values. On the first day of research for this book, I had arranged to interview Robert, a 69-year-old sales assistant at the Reading branch of a national retail group that has garnered acres of favourable publicity for its commitment to hiring older people. Five minutes before the interview was due to begin, Robert fainted and was taken to hospital in an ambulance. His sympathetic, but slightly exasperated manager filled in the background: 'Robert's a great guy, but he's now kicking into health problems.

This has now happened twice.' The manager gave a resigned shrug: 'When older people get ill, the illnesses seem a lot bigger and more complicated.'

It is easy to see the manager's point. Robert's health had clearly become a problem that was affecting his ability to work. On the other hand, the broad conclusion drawn by the manager about older people's health and general dependability is demonstrably false. Most research indicates that older workers are no more likely to take time off for illness than younger colleagues. Nor does their general physical and mental condition significantly impair their performance at work, according to Stephen McNair, director of the Centre for Research into the Older Workforce:

> There is no doubt that some physical and mental capacities decline with age. But in most jobs, most people find ways of working round this fact . . . As people get older, they simply get better at spotting short cuts. What also helps in a lot of jobs is the accumulation of know-how – of how to do the deal, and how to do it more efficiently.

The difficulty for older people is that many employers do not see them in this light. Indeed, the challenge for anyone wishing to sustain their careers past the current state pension ages of sixty for women and sixty-five for men really begins from about the age of fifty, when people start to be classified as 'old'. This is the low end of what most official statistical surveys count as the oldest age group in the 'working age' population, with the state pension ages taken as the upper limit.* The fifties are also the age range when numerous employers – consciously or not – begin to discriminate against older

---

* For instance, it is the definition used by the Office of National Statistics' Labour Force Survey.

staff. This discrimination can be explicit, such as passing over someone for promotion because his or her 'best years are behind them'. It can be more subtle, such as failing to enrol employees in their fifties on company training programmes, because they are assumed to be in the final phase of their careers, and so not worth the investment. At its worst, workplace ageism can lead to an employee over the age of fifty being shown the door, in order to make way for younger (and often cheaper) recruits straight out of school or college. For many people in the 50–64 age group, redundancy is a one-way street, because the chances of gaining another job sharply decrease after a person enters their fifties. While estimates vary, the government calculates there are up to one million people over the age of fifty who want to work but are unable to find employment.

Any discussion of the late shift therefore has to begin with the fact that people's employment prospects in their sixties are crucially affected by their career trajectory in the previous decade. It should be stressed that the overall employment outlook for the 50–64 age group is not entirely bleak, despite the large number of jobseekers in this cohort. From 1998 and 2006, the number of people in employment aged between fifty and sixty-four grew by 1.2 million. Yet this headline figure has to be set in context. About two-thirds of the total increase was simply due to the natural ageing of the population. And while the employment rate among people over fifty is rising faster than for any other cohort,* the overall proportion of this age group in work (71 per cent) is significantly less than for the

---

* For example, in the period May–July 2006, the number of people in work between aged fifty and the state pension age increased by 1.7 per cent. This rate of increase was more than double the equivalent figure for all other cohort samples below the state pension age (Labour Force Survey, Time Series Data 'Employment by Age', September 2006).

25–49 age group (81 per cent). That is of course to be expected, given that many people over fifty have taken early retirement. More worrying is the fact that the gap between the participation rates of these age groups in the workforce is wider than it was twenty-five years ago.

Such statistics expose the distance between the government's desire to boost the number of older people in work (by which it means people over fifty) and the intractable reality on the ground. The danger is that the wish of more older people to extend their careers will collide with a prevailing employment culture that still regards anyone approaching the state pension age as a wasting asset. Sue Yeandle, Professor of Sociology at the University of Leeds, concludes from her own research into older people and the workplace that most employers are barely out of the starting gates on the road to shedding their prejudices about age: 'We've still got this very strong cult of health and youth. We still think young is good. That's a very strong value in Western culture.'

The optimistic view, expressed by Lord Turner, is that the new age law may prove the catalyst that changes the prevailing corporate mindset about older workers. He argues that the law will not only force employers to treat older employees more fairly, but encourage a deeper change in business culture: 'I think the commentariat has probably underestimated what a big thing this is. It is going to make a big difference, and a very salutary difference.' His prediction is endorsed by Sam Mercer, director of the Employers Forum on Age, a British corporate lobbying group on age issues in the workplace whose members include such blue-chip firms as British Airways, the Royal Bank of Scotland and GlaxoSmithKline: 'I think most of our members now would say they support the legislation because it makes clear that ageism is unacceptable. It actually helps them generate activity within their organisations. They can get age taken much more seriously if they can use the stick that is the age legislation.'

There are, however, two reasons for believing that the impact of the age law will be limited, at least in the short term. The first is simply that the law *is* limited in scope. A ban on mandatory company retirement ages below sixty-five is a significant advance, but it is a long way from outlawing the system altogether. The second reason, as this crucial retreat illustrates, is that the government's lead on age and retirement issues during the run-up to the legislation has been feeble at best, and at times completely hypocritical. Its most indefensible U-turn came in October 2005, when Labour caved in to pressure from the big public sector unions and agreed to retain the right of civil servants, health and education workers who were currently on the central government payroll to retire at sixty on an index-linked, final-salary pension. In one back-door deal, Labour thus undercut the moral force of its case for raising the state pension age – that everyone should work longer before claiming a taxpayer-funded pension because of rising life expectancy and the consequent impact on the present system's affordability.

The government is therefore in no position to lecture the private sector – where about 80 per cent of Britain's workforce is employed – about the need to encourage older employees to extend their careers. And unfortunately, the business rationale for employing more older workers is rarely as self-evident as age campaigners suggest. For a start, companies that are geared towards meeting their next quarterly earning targets have little time to mull over the long-term consequences of an ageing society. Furthermore, those consequences have been partially mitigated in the medium term by the post-war baby boom, which has temporarily reduced the burden on the working-age population of supporting a growing number of older non-wealth creators. The old-age dependency ratio will rise sharply only after 2010, when the baby boomers, who have produced fewer children than their parents, begin to retire in force; and it will not be till about 2030 that the ratio reaches the trend level that would have occurred if there had been no baby boom between the late 1940s and the mid-1960s (see Figure 1.2).

Figure 1.2: Impact of the 1940s–1960s baby boom on the old-age dependency ratio in relation to the working-age population

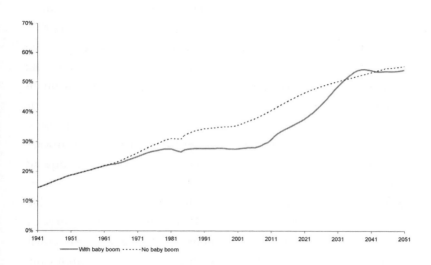

Source: *A New Pensions Settlement for the Twenty-First Century: Second Report of the Pensions Commission* (London: Pensions Commission, 2005), p. 5.
Note: Figures are for England and Wales only.

Even at this point, it is not clear that businesses will be under an urgent imperative to hire and retain more older employees to offset declining numbers of younger people entering the workforce. They could resort to using more migrant labour, as is already happening in a range of sectors that have attracted workers from the new EU member states in eastern Europe. Alternatively, they could relocate some operations to countries where there is an abundant, cheap supply of labour, according to Philip Taylor, Professor of Ageing and Social Policy at Swinburne University, Australia, and former director of the Cambridge Research Centre on Ageing:

> I could see a scenario where major global corporations, perceiving the ageing of their workforce and the labour market, will simply up sticks and move. Capital is chasing cheap labour, which is available in Asia, so why would business necessarily respond to the ageing of the population by recruiting older workers? I don't think we should necessarily buy into the view that an ageing population equates to ageing workers.

In reality, the employment prospects of older people who want (and in many instances, need) to extend their working lives depend on their ability to sell themselves to employers whose ultimate concern is the bottom line, not the wider social good. This point has often been lost in a debate about age discrimination in the workplace that has been dominated by politicians, policy think tanks, academics and campaign groups, with little substantive input from business beyond the CBI's rearguard defence of a default retirement age. It is a point, though, that is fully understood by people in the fifty-plus age group, who know from hard experience how the labour market operates.

For many people in their fifties and sixties, the challenge of finding and keeping a job involves a hard sell which will become only marginally easier as a result of the new age law. They confront a labour market made increasingly competitive by global economic forces, and a management mindset whose default mode regarding older people is epitomised by the remark of one HR director of a leading British firm with headquarters in Reading. When asked to defend his firm's 'normal' retirement age of sixty (with only the 'option' to carry on till sixty-five under the new age law), he responds: 'I think in some respects there are very good reasons why the retirement age is as it is . . . There is life after your working life, after all.'

The problem is that many older people either want or need to be part of that working life, for both personal and financial reasons, and do not see why employers should be allowed to impose an arbitrary finishing line for their careers. Such is the extent of the gap between a generation of greying baby boomers who are signing onto the late shift and a corporate world that still harks back to the days when company stalwarts automatically walked into the retirement sunset at a mandatory age with a shake of the managing director's hand.

*

This gap – and how to close it – is the subject of *Late Shift*. It attempts to capture a critical moment in British corporate life, when the presumption that a person's natural career span ended somewhere between sixty and sixty-five finally collapsed under the twin pressures of an ageing population and a looming pensions crisis. This book is not intended as an addition to the extensive academic and policy literature on the ageing workforce, though it draws on these sources. Instead, as a business journalist, I have viewed the question of whether employers can adapt to demographic change through the eyes of those most affected by the answer. They include executives who are wrestling (or not) with the implications of the new age law; older workers whose retirement is an ever-receding horizon; self-employed people in their fifties and sixties who have set up their own businesses at a time when many of their peers are winding down; and most depressingly, long-term unemployed people in the same age group with little prospect of ever returning to work.

Apart from their age, the connecting thread between over 100 people who agreed to be interviewed for this book is that they all work in and around Reading, my home town. Why the choice of Reading, a town of 144,000 people – with about the same number in the surrounding catchment area – forty miles west of London? Since the Second World War, Reading's ordinariness has made it a popular port of call for opinion pollsters and fly-on-the-wall television documentary producers in search of 'middle England'. Yet Reading is distinctive in two ways that make it an ideal base for observing Britain's late shift. Firstly, local people work for a wide range of employers, from high-tech multinationals such as Oracle and Microsoft (both of whose European headquarters are located in Reading), through major British corporate names such as John Lewis and Prudential, to dozens of small, family-owned businesses and shops – many of which are run by first- and second-generation immigrants. Reading also has a substantial public sector, centred on the borough council, the hospital, the main university and the nearby atomic weapons research establishment at Aldermaston. It is, in short, an excellent laboratory for testing the attitudes of employers to older workers.

Secondly, Reading is relatively prosperous, and suitably qualified workers are in high demand. In 2005, the town's official unemployment rate was 4.4 per cent, slightly below the national rate.* According to Jean Charmak, owner of Forest, a local recruitment

---

* *Labour Market Profile: Reading* (Durham: Nomis, 2005).

agency, Reading's companies are awash with vacancies: 'Every one of my people will say they have got jobs they can't fill because they can't find the people with the right skills.' In theory, therefore, Reading ought to be a welcoming place for resourceful older people who want to carry on working through their sixties and perhaps into their seventies.

The reality is more complex, including numerous examples of blatant age discrimination (see Box 1.1).

Box 1.1: Ian and Pat Reed – able, willing and unwelcome

Ian Reed, 59, and his wife Pat, 58, came back to England in 1999 after spending most of their lives in Zimbabwe. They settled in Reading, and while both of them had British passports, they had no illusions about the difficulty of finding work. However, both were soon employed. Ian, a former sales and marketing executive, got a job as a resources manager at a girls' private school in Reading. Meanwhile, Pat was hired as a secretary at the Reading offices of Thales, the French defence and electronics multinational.

Their luck changed in 2004 when Pat was made redundant following a corporate restructuring. Eight months later, Ian also lost his job as a result of cost-cutting. Since then, neither has found permanent work, and they both testify to rampant ageism at the recruitment agencies where they have registered. Ian says: 'I had a telephone interview with one of them and we went through this thing for about ten minutes and I thought it was going swimmingly . . . We were laughing and joking with each other, and then towards the end of the conversation she [the recruiter] said: "I notice that you haven't put your age on your CV. As a matter of interest, how old are you?" So I told her, and you could almost hear the shutters coming down. She said, "Well, we've got nothing at the moment, I'm afraid, and I'll be in touch," and she put the phone down.'

> Pat nods in agreement. 'This is what all the agencies say: "Don't put your age on your CV." I've been for several permanent positions, and I've been second choice and been told I was very close to getting the job. And I have that feeling that all along they had no idea how old I was until I actually appeared for the interview.'

The often frustrating experience of older people in Reading's labour market points to a particularly hard lesson for this age group to learn. Ultimately, it is their strength of character, far more than any external factors, that has most influence on their employment prospects.

During the early stages of research, two encounters highlighted this point, which became a recurring theme in all the interviews. The first took place at Sainsbury's hypermarket in Calcot, a suburb on the western edge of Reading. Sainsbury's chief executive, Justin King, had recently launched a new initiative to recruit older workers, and the Calcot store had arranged for me to meet some of its more 'mature' employees. One of them was Anne Murch, the 69-year-old deputy manager of the supermarket's petrol station. As she briskly recapped the details of her life, it became apparent that Anne's varied career had depended on large reserves of self-discipline and willpower.

Anne was born in east London, and married her first husband, Bill, in 1957. They both worked for her father's aluminium stockholding business, opening branches in various locations in south-east England. Their last store was in Purley-on-Thames, near Reading, where Anne looked after the back office and Bill dealt with the customers. But in 1967, with two small children, 'my marriage packed up'. Bill stayed with the aluminium firm, while Anne signed up with Pippa Dee, a direct sales company that sold women's and children's clothes across south-east England.

During the late 1960s and early 1970s Anne worked as a sales rep for Pippa Dee in the Berkshire area. Meanwhile, she met and married her second husband, Jim, and settled down again. However, in 1978 Anne's life took a further unexpected turn when the economy stalled and Jim's business almost collapsed. 'He came home one day and said, "I'm going off to Saudi Arabia." So off he went and I followed him about ten months later.'

Anne and Jim spent six happy years in Saudi Arabia, where he worked for an American civil engineering company. Then in 1984 two disasters struck:

> My husband unfortunately got cancer and had an operation in Dhahran. We went home [to England] for convalescence and then came back to Saudi Arabia. And ten days after coming back, the company went down. At that point the cancer was back, and it was going through Jim's kidneys. He went to bed and never got up again. Over there, women weren't allowed a passport, weren't allowed to drive, weren't allowed to work. So I had, somehow, to get us out of the country . . . I sold all the furniture in the villa to get money, and of course all the moneys that were in the company that were owed to us – it was about £50,000–£60,000 in those days – went. It just disappeared.
>
> So eventually I managed to get home, and Jim went straight into hospital and died a month later . . . I had to start life all over again. At the age of forty-eight, I was really, really desperate.

By this time, Anne's son and daughter had grown up, with her son going to work in the family's aluminium stockholding firm. Short of options, Anne returned to Pippa Dee, where her new job was to 'recruit, train and motivate' the women in the Berkshire sales network:

They retired you at fifty-eight. They gave you a set of targets and I had to get to £500,000 and then we'd get a huge big silver disc. And that last year I got to £498,000-and-something, and I thought the pressure was really on, and they were going to retire me anyway. So I thought the best thing to do was to stand down and end at the top. I was top district in the country.

Did she resent being retired at fifty-eight?

'To a degree I did, because being on my own, obviously, I have to be money motivated. But again, with sales jobs the pressure is very, very intense. Although I was disappointed that it happened, in the end I went through it, and looked forward.'

With no savings, and only a small state pension in prospect, Anne needed to carry on working. She decided to improve her job chances by enrolling on a computer course, mindful of the fact that in her days of managing the office at the aluminium company, everything had still been filed on paper.

And then out of the blue, my first husband retired – this was originally my father's business – and my son rang me and said, 'Would you like to come and work with us, Mum?' So I went back and worked for this aluminium stockholder for a year, which I absolutely adored. And then, blow me down, a big company in Leeds came and took us over, and my son, who was the managing director, he decided he didn't want to work for this new company, and of course, they didn't want his mum any more.

I was just coming up to my sixty-first birthday. I was without a job, with no pension or anything like that, and I thought, 'What will I do?'

Anne's immediate solution was to attend a recruitment day at Sainsbury's hypermarket in Calcot. Sainsbury's said her age was no problem, and she started straightaway on the tills. From there, she rapidly worked her way up to the position of assistant store manager. 'Then about four years ago they asked me if I'd like to run the petrol station, and I said, "Oh, I'm too old." And they said, "No, no, we think you can do it."'

A few months before our meeting, Anne had voluntarily chosen to step down one rank to be deputy manager of the petrol station. 'It's an awful lot of pressure and I'm sixty-nine years old . . . I just felt I wanted a bit more quality of life.' For the same reason, Anne was also wondering whether to leave Sainsbury's altogether, but she still was not ready for retirement. 'Even now, I sometimes think, "Oh God, at sixty-nine, will I be able to go out there again?" but I think I could. I really think I could.'

Faced with a series of setbacks in middle age, Anne's management of her later career had been exemplary. She had been hard-working, flexible, willing to learn new skills and, in the case of Sainsbury's, prepared to downsize initially to a junior checkout job in order to get herself back into work. In this respect, she fitted a profile shared by many capable older women, according to Stephen McNair:

> It's in the nature of what women's employment has been like over the last thirty or forty years. Most [older] women have had periods of not working. They've been in and out of work, and they've also had periods of part-time working . . . whereas most men in their sixties did grow up in a world where the assumption was full-time employment for forty years. I think women of this generation didn't see work like that, so it's less of a shock when they realise they have got to move on and rethink their role.

A week after interviewing Anne I met Don, a redundant 59-year-old computer software developer. The contrast in terms of character could not have been greater.

Don was a regular at a job club for unemployed people over fifty organised by the Reading Training Employment Advice Shop (TEA Shop), an advice centre partly financed by the local council. A wiry man with a drooping Mexican moustache, Don exuded gloom about his prospects of ever getting back into work. In 2004, he had been laid off by a company that produced computerised psychometric assessment programs, and had been unemployed ever since. On this day, his defeatism seemed contagious, as the other three members of the job club – all unemployed men – were demoralised by a series of sardonic remarks by Don about the poor quality of their CVs. Yet on paper, Don was the least hopeless case of the quartet. As Mike Coulson, the resolutely upbeat organiser of the club observed, Don's inability to find a job seemed a mystery, given his comparatively accomplished CV.

The mystery unravelled several months later when I met Don again at his bungalow in Woodley, on the eastern outskirts of Reading. Don was friendly and welcoming, but it was no surprise to hear that he was still unemployed. Lighting the first of many cigarettes, he recounted a lengthy – and lengthening – hard-luck story.

His first marriage had ended in divorce many years before, and Don had subsequently lost touch with one of his two daughters. He was now happily remarried, but in the meantime, Don's once-promising career had gone off the rails.

Don's first experience of redundancy had been in 1996, when he lost his long-standing job in the technology division of a multinational construction firm:

It was the beginning of November, and I felt I'd got to get a job before Christmas, because nothing was going to happen over Christmas, and I hadn't had an interview for the best part of thirty years. But because I'd had three months' salary in lieu of notice, the Job Centre didn't want to know anything for about three months. At the end of the three months I was still out of work, so I phoned them then. I was just fifty at the time. And then I was down at the Job Centre every week, and I had to fill in a little diary saying what you had done. It got very hassling.

Don's dismissive attitude towards government support networks for unemployed people dated from this episode.

I never got anything out of it, and one of [the Job Centre staff] said to me, 'Well, have you tried looking at anything else?' And I said, 'You show me where your IT job board is, and I'll look at it.' I looked at the notice board, and the jobs that were advertised were in catering or whatever.

In 1998, at the height of the technology boom, Don finally got a job with the company that produced psychometric tests. In 2002, following a takeover, he had the option of either becoming an employee of the acquiring company and moving to its headquarters in west London, or staying in Windsor with his former company (now a subsidiary) on his existing contract. He chose to stay, because his former company had a better redundancy package than the new one. Don's pessimism about his job security was justified. In July 2004, with no end in sight to a four-year technology slump, he was made redundant. 'There was an annual cull. It wasn't me particularly. It had happened every year since I'd got there.'

Don had never stopped trying to get back into employment since losing his job, which had paid him an annual salary of £42,000. He estimated that he had applied for about sixty vacancies, mostly through various online technology recruitment agencies where he was registered. Yet despite a general recovery in the sector, he had always been rejected. Don had several explanations for why his job search was getting nowhere:

> I suppose that software is definitely a bit of a young man's game nowadays, and it's very, very fast moving. I did an HNC [Higher National Certificate] between 1985 and 1987 and nothing I was taught then really bears any relevance to today's world. Another possibility might be that I've never worked in a formal software house environment . . . Over the last six years, I was the only software developer in the company, so I didn't get to bounce ideas off anyone. I tended to lose out a little on the latest technologies.

Don was sceptical about whether he could make himself more employable by upgrading his IT skills because, as he observed, 'it's a question of what you want to upgrade to'. Armed with this paralysing insight, Don still ran Windows 98 on his own computer, even though he was trying to sell himself to high-tech companies with advanced software systems.

Don had at least considered downsizing to a less well-paid job in another sector. But all he could see were obstacles in his path:

> I'm reasonably competent at DIY and that sort of thing, and I thought maybe I could get into plumbing or be an electrician. But of course, with your average vacancy, you've got to have qualifications and with some of these things you can take two years or more on a course . . . And then I thought I'd have a look on the [Job Centre's] general job site. And even looking at fairly menial jobs, they're still

looking for some experience. About the only ones where you can get a job that doesn't involve experience is in caring, which is definitely not me.

After an hour listening to Don, it was tempting to tell him that he had an attitude problem. Unlike Anne, he seemed bent on making himself as unattractive as possible to a potential future employer. Despite a friendly nature, he was inflexible, dogmatic and, as his negative view of the job club demonstrated, almost impossible to help: 'I find it a bit depressing, to be honest, a bit like Alcoholics Anonymous. You know, it's like you say, "My name's Don, I'm unemployed." And everyone says, "Well done, you've owned up."'

There are, of course, hard-luck cases like Don in every age group. But his obstinate refusal to make himself more employable seems especially foolish for someone of his age, given the widespread prejudice that older jobseekers confront. It is true that at the bottom end of the labour market there are older people who display a remarkable facility for muddling from one low-paid job to the next, despite a general unsuitability for any kind of employment. Yet even at this level, employers are becoming more demanding about the kind of people they hire (see Box 1.2). For example, supermarket chains now routinely require applicants for lowly customer service jobs to complete online aptitude and personality tests before they are considered for an interview – thus screening out candidates who lack basic literacy and computer skills.

Box 1.2: Roy, the survivor whose time is up
Roy, a loquacious, volatile 56-year-old Irishman, has spent much of his career proving that even the most unreliable type can find work in an affluent town like Reading. In the past two years, however, his luck as a serial jobhopper has finally run out.

Roy came to Britain from Limerick in 1966 to work as an apprentice aircraft engineer. Within a few months he left for a better-paid job in Slough with Mars, the confectionery company, and then moved to Reading to run an off-licence. In 1984, tired of the drinks trade, Roy became a postman. Meanwhile, his first marriage had ended in divorce, and in 1989 his second marriage also broke down. 'When your first marriage goes down the pan, you think, "Oh well, tough." When the second one goes down the pan, you think, "Hang on, there must be something wrong here." And I went off the rails. I know I did.'

Roy's drinking got heavier, and in 1993, after three drink-driving offences and the loss of his post office job, he was jailed for a month. He smiles ruefully: 'Once you put that on your CV it gets fairly difficult to get a job.' Yet Roy's next employer seems to have been oblivious to his drink problems. In 1994 he was hired as a 'liquor supervisor' in the alcoholic drinks section of a leading discount supermarket in Reading. In 1998 he fell out with his manager there and became a security guard. This job lasted for three years, until he broke his kneecap in an accident at work and sued the security firm for compensation. He was then briefly a warehouse storeman, before joining another security group. In 2002 he was fired after someone at the company he was guarding complained about his conduct. 'I didn't know what I had done. Who had I upset? Give me a reason why. I drove myself into a depression. I ended up spending three weeks on the sofa, only getting up to have a drink of water or to go to the toilet.'

Roy eventually went back to work with yet another security firm, but was soon protesting about the long hours. In 2003, after receiving generous compensation for his original kneecap injury, he resigned and decamped to Malta for several months 'on sabbatical'.

In the summer of 2004, Roy returned to Reading. For the next ten months he survived on the rest of his compensation money, plus his partner, whose home provides him with rent-free accommodation. In April 2005 he signed on at the Job Centre, but almost immediately landed a position with another high street retailer that was recruiting staff for its outlet at Paddington station, half an hour by train from Reading. This job lasted a month before Roy was dismissed. 'It ended up with a very strange set of circumstances. I went to collect the change for the day and came under suspicion of stealing £100 from the safe. There were various other complaints, such as my breath smelling of drink – basically because I was using mouthwash, because my gums were sore.'

Roy was initially upbeat about his prospects of finding more work; after all, he had always found job-hunting a doddle. But in the summer of 2006 he was still unemployed, having been rejected (according to him) for more than 100 positions. He blames everyone but himself, and says he is still game for anything, with only one no-go zone: 'I won't do bar work. I wouldn't mind bar management, though.'

Older people therefore face multiple pressures when they compete for jobs in the modern labour market, which to a large extent only they can resolve. They have to be sufficiently smart and personable to outshine much younger applicants. They must overcome ageist prejudices which will only be partially mitigated by the new legislation. And they may be applying for a vacancy, or clinging onto a job, in the knowledge that it could be their last chance to stay in employment and eventually receive a decent pension.

Should an unemployed 56-year-old manual worker take a low-paid shelf-stacking job at one of Reading's many supermarkets, or hope that a better-paid factory job becomes vacant at a company that is genuinely age blind? Does a highly qualified 53-year-old computer programmer take a risk when he is made redundant and launch his own corporate website design business? And how can a 59-year-old female executive balance the need to care for sick and elderly relatives with a demanding job as a purchasing manager with a large British company? These are some of the dilemmas faced by individuals in the following six chapters, which describe the world of work in Reading as it appears to local people in the fifty-plus age group.

As Chapter 2 illustrates, early career memories have been critical in shaping this generation's attitude to work. During their lifetime, Reading's economy has changed dramatically, in line with the rest of Britain and western Europe. In Chapters 3 to 6, the book explores the contrasting fortunes of older people in an employment landscape that has been transformed by three trends in particular: the emergence of a booming retail sector; the impact of globalisation; and the decline of the old world of unskilled manual work. Chapter 7 investigates the situation of older women in Reading, many of whom did not pay their full national insurance contribution and now face a serious pension shortfall. The tour of Reading concludes by comparing the experiences of older public sector employees, whose generous final-salary index-linked pensions seem utterly unjust to most of their private sector counterparts.

It would be good to report that in one, relatively well-off English town, the changes in the treatment of older workers urged by governments throughout the developed world are well underway. The reality on the ground is less hopeful. Reading's labour market is a tough, competitive environment, where businesses recruit in order to drive up profits rather than promote the general welfare. It is a place, in short, where any older person who needs to extend their working life must be prepared for a very hard sell.

2   Beer, biscuits and bulbs

Pete Dunne has happy memories of his first job in 1955 as a packer at the Huntley & Palmers biscuit factory in Reading: 'I used to love the smell of the biscuits when it rained. The dampness in the air – it always got to me. It was a lovely place to work. That's when people cared a little bit more about people. Not like today; it's all money, money, money.'

A gregarious 65-year-old grandfather, Pete has spent all his life in Reading. He regrets how the convivial workplace of the 1950s and 1960s has gradually disappeared from his home town:

> Places all used to have their own clubs. Once a year, the oldies would come at Christmas time and get a free Christmas dinner and they could all use that club the rest of the year to have a drink and see their mates or whatever. That doesn't exist today, does it? So I don't think the fear of retiring was as bad as it is today, because the fear of retirement is being lonely. And when they had their little circle of friends and their social clubs, you could go out and have a pint, and there'd always be somebody in there. But today, I think, once you're retired, you're isolated, that's it. [See Box 2.1]

Box 2.1: Joan Mason – counting her blessings

Not everyone subscribes to the view that retirement is the loneliest age. Joan Mason looks back fondly on the post-retirement years that she shared with her late husband Bill, whose photograph takes pride of place on the mantelpiece of her small house in Tilehurst, west Reading. She and Bill met during the Second World War, when they both worked at the old Simonds brewery, which was eventually acquired by Courage in 1960.

Bill retired from the brewery in 1990 at the age of sixty-five and took a part-time job as a school bus driver in villages on the Berkshire–Hampshire border. 'I was his escort,' says Joan. 'We had a lovely run, all through the country. We didn't touch any main roads. But in the end he went into hospital for a spell, and he said, "I don't think I can carry on." So I carried on till I was sixty-eight and then they made me redundant.'

Bill eventually died in 2004 but Joan – now seventy-nine – is still active socially as a member of the Tilehurst branch of the Townswomen's Guild. 'My gran, when she was an old age pensioner, she never did anything. She just used to sit and listen to the radio. And once a week she'd go and visit her daughter down in Great Knollys Street [in central Reading] . . . She never went anywhere. With me, I can go on trips to the sea, I can go on holiday. I'm busy.'

Joan's sunny nature illustrates how a person's temperament often plays a key role in determining attitudes to work and retirement, regardless of material circumstances. She does not have much of an income, even though the mortgage has been paid off on her home, which she shares with her only son, her daughter-in-law and two grandchildren. After a career spent hopping from one clerical job to the next, she has no pension of her own, relying instead on the widow's pension she receives from Courage, worth about £20 per week, and just under £100 per week from her state pension. Her only other source of income is occasional 'pocket money' when she works as a presiding officer at local and general elections.

Many people in Joan's position would grumble about making ends meet. Joan takes the opposite view: 'My friends' children say they're going to get a certain pension when they finish which is an awful lot. But to me, I think, £20 from Courage, and then there's £7 a week in pension credit, and then the state pension is nearly £100 a week – that's not bad, you know. So I think I'm quite well off.'

Pete is determined to put off that evil day. After Huntley & Palmers, he spent twenty years as an engineer at BT, and retired at the company's (then) mandatory age of sixty with a final-salary pension. As he explains, he does not need to work for the money. Nonetheless, since leaving BT he has taken several part-time jobs, principally for social reasons. Most recently, he has been working weekday mornings as a sales assistant at the Reading branch of B&Q, the home improvement retail chain. He particularly likes this job, because he meets people who would not normally cross his radar screen. 'The people here are blooming great. There's one chap here who's twenty-one who said, "I didn't think I'd get on with old people, but it's turned out a treat."'

Like many older working-class people in Reading, Pete's attitude to employment was shaped by his early career experiences in the 1950s and 1960s. At this time, Reading's corporate landscape was still dominated by the so-called 'Three Bs': the beer produced at the Courage brewery in the middle of town on a site by the river Kennet; the biscuits made half a mile downstream at another riverside location by Huntley & Palmers; and the bulbs grown by Suttons Seeds, one of Britain's leading horticultural firms, on nursery grounds where the Kennet meets the river Thames. The Three Bs each had local roots stretching back to the nineteenth century, and offered relatively secure, steady employment to many of Reading's unskilled and semi-skilled workers. And if you could not get a job at one of the Three Bs, there were usually vacancies for assembly line work at Gillette, another leading manufacturer in Reading, which opened a large factory on the Basingstoke Road in 1947 producing shaving cream, shampoo and personal care products.

This stable industrial scene instilled several common and long-standing assumptions about work among local people who entered Reading's labour force during the twenty years after the Second World War. Firstly, as Pete's example demonstrates, work was seen as an extension of social life, compensating for the fact that the job itself was often fairly dull. Sally Greengross, director of the International Longevity Centre, a London-based research group, and former head of the charity Age Concern, says Pete is correct to identify the loneliness of retired life for many people as a major reason for continuing to work: 'However boring it was on an assembly line or in a biscuit factory, at least you had friends to chat to. That's why [retired] people go back and work on the cash till at the supermarket, because at least there's mates you can talk to and you're not isolated.'

Secondly, there was a widespread perception among many Reading workers of this generation that company managers, however remote, cared about their employees' general welfare. Mick Pollek, who joined Courage in 1972, remembers a corporate culture that harked back to the Victorian era:

> They would have annually a family fun day, where there would be a tug of war, management against the workers. Now in those days the head brewer had a bowler hat and people would salute him. They hired a whole train to go down to Margate – all free, all for families. The kids were given doggy bags and the old man had his bottle of beer.

These jaunts were the residue of a Victorian tradition of corporate social responsibility that found expression in Britain at the end of the nineteenth century in the garden villages of Port Sunlight, built near Liverpool by William Hesketh Lever for his soap factory workers, and Bournville, a residential development in Birmingham for employees of the Cadbury's chocolate firm. Similar values informed the workplace culture of patrician employers in Europe such as the Michelin brothers at Clermont-Ferrand in France and the Philips family at Eindhoven in the Netherlands.

In Reading, as elsewhere, this corporate ethos is still regarded fondly by company veterans. Mick spent thirty years at Courage, where he was heavily involved in the brewery branch of the Transport & General Workers' Union (TGWU). He is now full-time head of the regional branch of the TGWU. Yet as a union man, he is surprisingly positive about the traditional us-and-them corporate hierarchy at the brewery: 'There was, I suppose, a kind of paternalistic approach at Courage. But in turn, its staff worked and delivered.'

Such comments reflect a third assumption about the nature of work shared by many Reading people before the government of Margaret Thatcher overturned the post-war social contract in the 1980s. They thought that both management and workers owed each other their loyalty. Ray Buckland still believes strongly in this implicit understanding. Now fifty-eight, Ray joined Courage at the age of seventeen and has stayed there ever since, rising to become a material controls manager responsible for cans and bottles.

> I consider it to be a two-way street. I joined as a labourer and they've given me a good living. And in return I've worked hard, and I think they've had a good deal out of me . . . It's a bit over the top to say that when I walked into the company I only had the clothes on my back,

but I didn't have an awful lot more. Now I have a house, a car, and we have holidays; that's all come because I've worked thirty-nine years for the brewery.

It is true, of course, that such early workplace memories are often heavily rose tinted. During the 1960s and early 1970s, when Courage was still organising seaside outings for its workers, managers were spending much of the rest of the year dealing with intractable labour disputes. Down the river Kennet at Huntley & Palmers, the atmosphere was not all laughs and drinks at the social club. Marie Webb, now sixty-one, recalls joining Huntley & Palmers as an office clerk in the early 1960s:

> You had a very strict boss in Huntley & Palmers, very strict. You had to toe the line. You had to go to work dressed properly. You had an overall, but you had to have very low-heeled shoes or flat shoes, with tights, and your hair had to be tied back.

Furthermore, as Pete Dunne concedes, Huntley & Palmers' own brand of Victorian paternalism did not extend to offering a company-wide pension scheme: 'In those days, if you didn't work in the office, you didn't get a pension. So we'd be relying on a state pension.' Yet souvenirs of the best of the old world of employment, rather than the more dreary, hierarchical reality, still serve as a guide for how work ought to be among many Reading people who entered the labour force in the 1950s and 1960s.

This past vanished from Reading during the economic upheaval of the 1970s and 1980s. The decline of manufacturing in the town was marked physically by the disappearance of two of the Three Bs. Huntley & Palmers ceased trading as an independent business in 1969, when it merged with two other firms to form Associated

Biscuits. Biscuit-making ended in Reading in 1976, and in 1989 the Victorian redbrick Huntley & Palmers factory was demolished and replaced by an office complex for the Prudential insurance group. Meanwhile, Suttons Seeds relocated to Paignton in Devon in 1976, following the announcement of plans to carve a dual carriageway through its main plantation grounds. Only the last of the Bs, brewing, still remains in Reading, with the Courage brand now part of the Scottish & Newcastle group. In 1985 the brewery moved to a new site on the town's southern outskirts, close to the M4 motorway. All the original brewery buildings were knocked down, apart from a grain store, which was converted into a restaurant, and the old management office on Bridge Street.

*

The new Reading of shopping complexes, office plazas and high-tech business parks that emerged in the 1990s also spelt an end to the old certainties about a job – or jobs – for life (see Box 2.2). Today, in a more competitive local economy, there is no such thing as guaranteed employment. Instead, Reading's job market is unforgiving to workers of any age who do not have the necessary technical and personal skills.

Box 2.2: Clive – cast adrift by the new job market

Clive, 59, has spent most of his career moving from one manual job to the next, safe in the knowledge that he would never have trouble finding work in Reading's buoyant labour market. A steady, dependable type, he argues convincingly (unlike Roy – see Box 1.2) that he has always given his many employers value for his wage packet. But in the past four years, Clive has descended into a bewildering, stressful world of permanent unemployment.

His initial mistake, at the age of fifty-five, was to hand in his notice as a general storeman for a newspaper and magazine distributor in Reading. 'I was a little bit too helpful, so I would fill in if there was a gap. I would do it, and I got paid for it, so I just wore myself into the ground doing nights. And the nights turned into days, and at the end of it I'd just had a bit too much. So basically, I just said "that's it", because the same people were going home early or off sick or couldn't be relied upon to do the job.'

Clive thought it would be easy to find another manual position, given his previous experience of job-hunting. Born in Reading, he had done stints over the years as a fork lift driver, packer, porter, chauffeur and general handyman for local companies ranging from a firm that made pumps to a bakery. 'Jobs were so plentiful. When I was a young man, I felt if I wanted a change I just went for it.'

Four years after walking out of his last job, Clive is still baffled by the countless rejections he has received from other employers: 'I put in four applications only this morning. It's not always as many as that . . . I've listed skills, skills, skills all the way down. I've loads of them, to be quite honest. I'm reliable, dependable, I'm self-motivated, courteous, enquiring, and try to do the best I can for the job. And if I see a possibility of doing it better, I might suggest it.'

Clive's main problem is that his skills have not kept pace with economic development in Reading. He is wary of computers and resents the increasing insistence by companies that job applications should be sent by e-mail. 'With application forms, everything needs to go online . . . I think providing your handwriting's legible and you can put yourself across confidently, and you can listen – I think these are basic skills that you do need to know. If you go along solely on the lines of being online, we're going to lose some of these qualities.'

Clive also feels threatened by the waves of immigrants who have arrived in Reading since his youth, some of whom are now his neighbours in the high-rise council block where he lives on his own: 'When you get to my sort of age you feel that you're just chucked aside, when the country just opens up the door and says, "Oh, you can come over if you're from Poland, you can come over if you're from Africa. Come on." Brilliant. And they're laughing.'

The more Clive talks, the more he seems marooned by Reading's new economy. He has just failed a psychometric test for a job as a shelf stacker at the Reading branch of a big national retailer – the reliable fallback for cheerier types like Pete Dunne (see text). Yet as he churns out more application forms, Clive remains doggedly upbeat about the chances that someone, somewhere, will eventually hire him: 'I've got to be optimistic. I can't afford not to be . . . Anyone can look back, and there are certain things in their life I would imagine they regret. But that's not the way forward. That just holds you back further.'

This point is underlined by Sue Culver, who runs one of the over-fifty job clubs at the local TEA Shop: 'I try to change their attitude and the way they are looking for work, because it isn't the same as it was years ago. You could see a postcard go in the window, someone would apply, and there'd be no other applicants. The employer would say, "Can you start next week? Great, we'll have you."'

But it is not just traditional blue-collar workers who risk being stranded in Reading's new economy. The same national and international economic forces have undermined the job security of a whole tier of middle managers who imagined their positions were as solid as the town's Victorian industrial architecture. They can only look enviously at colleagues in the same 50–65 age group who – through a mixture of luck and judgement – have been able to retire early on lavish final-salary pensions. Companies across Britain are now racing to close these defined-benefits pension schemes in order to cap soaring deficits.

Yet there is a large class of beneficiaries who have in effect escaped all the late career worries of their peers. Lord Turner says:

> The problem is that we have simply ended up with some inequalities which are totally arbitrary. There are a lot of people who are retiring right now with what are going to look in retrospect like absolutely golden pensions. The high-salary person who is retiring today aged sixty with a fully indexed final-salary pension is going to be looked back on in thirty years time as golden-age stuff.

Jim Thorpe, a 57-year-old former sales team manager at Gillette's Reading factory, is a good example of a middle-income employee with the luck to have been working for the right company at the right time. He retired from Gillette in February 2006 after twenty-five years with the company on an index-linked pension that pays him 'about 60 per cent' of his final salary. Relaxed and permanently suntanned, Jim divides his time between the villa he and his wife have bought near Benidorm and their home in Reading.

> It sounds bad, doesn't it, retiring at fifty-seven and doing nothing. But I think we've put in a lot of effort and time while we've been working . . . And I just feel now that with all the things that are going on in the world, you never know, you might not be here in a few years' time. So therefore I'd like to spend a few years enjoying it.

The workplace Jim has left behind is rife with white-collar insecurity. Gillette's distinctive redbrick factory on Reading's Basingstoke Road, crowned by a clock tower, used to be a seemingly immovable local corporate landmark. At its peak in the 1960s and 1970s, the factory employed around 600 people to produce and package most of Gillette's shaving cream, shampoo and personal care products for the European market. But in recent years several production lines have been closed, and the workforce has shrunk to about 250 employees. Meanwhile, the factory has been shaken by two events far from Reading. In 2004, Gillette announced plans to shut down its other main British manufacturing plant in Isleworth, west London, and transfer production to Poland, where labour costs are cheaper. The fear in Reading, not yet realised, is that the factory will suffer the same fate as Isleworth. Then in 2005, Gillette was taken over by Procter & Gamble, the US personal hygiene and household products multinational, which immediately launched a cost-cutting programme to achieve promised post-merger savings. In Reading, the first casualties of this streamlining process are a clutch of middle managers.

Ian Little, a 57-year-old maintenance supervisor, is still stunned by the recent news that his job is being eliminated:

> I'm in a really strange position at the moment, because my job has just been made redundant. It was amalgamated with the job of stores coordinator, which I had to apply for, and I didn't get it . . . I now have the option of departing or applying for a job in tools, which is where I came from six years ago . . . So I'm really torn at the moment. There's a huge part of me that wants to tell them to take the job and do what they want with it, and I'll go my own way. But the sensible part of me tells me that for every year I stay here I will increase my pension.

Ian's sense of betrayal is all the greater because his roots are firmly planted in the old world of a steady career leading to a secure retirement. 'I'm probably quite boring really, but I don't like change for the sake of change. I've only had five jobs since I left school.'

The son of a policeman, Ian was born in west London and moved with his wife to Reading in the 1960s. Until 1988 he worked at Huntley, Boorne & Stevens, a now-defunct Reading biscuit tin manufacturer that was founded by another member of the Huntley dynasty. Ian gradually became disenchanted with his job, especially after 1985, when Huntley, Boorne & Stevens was acquired by a rival packaging company. His move to Gillette in 1988 coincided with his wife returning to full-time employment after a period bringing up their two children. For a while, the Littles' future looked secure. Ian enjoyed his job at Gillette, while his wife landed a good job in the accounts department of a sports car manufacturer.

Ian's worries began after the stock market slump of 2000–1, when he realised that his potential retirement income would be insufficient to sustain his lifestyle. His first corporate pension was with Huntley & Palmers, the parent company of Huntley, Boorne & Stevens. Ian decided to take the capital he had accumulated and start an endowment policy with Pearl, the insurance group. When he got his job at Gillette, he also joined the company's final-salary pension scheme (now closed). Ian calculated that if he stayed with Gillette for about twenty years, the combined income from both pension pots would finance a comfortable retirement.

Unfortunately the stock markets have put paid to that. So I will probably have to work on till retirement to give myself a reasonable standard of living . . . I have a huge shortfall on both counts [Pearl and Gillette], which is pushing the retirement plan that I once had further and further into the distance. I feel aggrieved that you can take all the advice at the time, and you buy your endowment from the best company and you buy your pension with the best company and then they sell you out. I sometimes wonder if there's somebody out there who's determined to keep me poor.

The news that his job was being cut thus came at the worst possible time, because Ian had been counting on Gillette to see him through till he was sixty-five. Now that his prospects are uncertain, he is trying to gauge his marketability.

I'd convinced myself that at the age of fifty-seven I was probably unsellable. I've now found in the last two months that that is not true. I think I will probably have to rethink the salary side of things . . . If somebody walked through that door now and said to me, 'We can offer you a job which is going to be £3,000–£4,000 less than you're getting, but you're just the person we want,' then I would have to seriously think about going. Purely from the fact that I'm so fed up at the moment. My wife said to me last night that if you really are getting that depressed, you ought to go, because you're not doing yourself any favours.

Ian is also dubious about the wisdom of swallowing his pride and applying for his old job in the tools department:

My other major fear is going through all this pain and grief, making the decision to stay, and then two years down the line Gillette saying, 'We're going to move manufacturing to Poland.' And then I'll be two years older. At fifty-seven I don't consider myself old. But when you start saying fifty-nine or sixty, maybe you haven't got many years to give somebody, have you?

The shock of redundancy is proportionately greater for people in Ian's fifty-plus age group, according to Stephen McNair, director of the Centre for Research into the Older Workforce:

Those of us who are now in our fifties grew up in a world where redundancy didn't happen. It was almost unknown. For some it was a moral blot, and for others it was a very distressing, worrying experience. If you look at people now in their thirties, the experience of redundancy is much more common.

As Ian realises, the only way forward is to pick himself up and find another job. But McNair points out that such a challenge is especially daunting for a demoralised person on the wrong side of fifty in a society where age discrimination is rife: 'People over fifty who have been made redundant seem to end up fairly consistently on the bottom end of the choices in the post-fifty labour market.'

At the heart of the predicament of older, frequently well-qualified jobseekers is a seeming contradiction. On the one hand, they can fall back on a support network of skills and training agencies, government programmes and job clubs that did not exist at the start of their careers. On the other hand, the old qualities (real or imagined) of solidarity and loyalty between employer and employed are rarely found in the modern labour market. The outcome for many older people who are thrown out of work is the isolating sense that they are on their own in an unfamiliar, hostile landscape without a map to guide them.

Dana Molecki has experienced the loneliness of trying to rebuild a career on the 'wrong side' of fifty. Now fifty-seven, Dana took her first unexpected turn in life in her early forties, when her marriage broke down and she got divorced. Until then, she had been happy raising her only son, doing occasional part-time secretarial work, and helping her husband with his picture-framing business from their home in rural south Oxfordshire. 'I realised that the marriage was ending and that I needed to earn what I call a proper salary rather than be dependent on part-time work plus the husband's income.'

Dana initially took a part-time position as the assistant to the regional director of a charitable housing trust. As a newly single woman, she was determined to improve her office skills on the job, and soon she was hired on a full-time basis. Three years later, she moved up another level when she became PA to the managing director of a small joint venture in Newbury, twenty miles west of Reading. 'I wasn't entirely happy there, but I'd made a good step because this joint venture was actually a start-up, and I was gaining huge amounts of experience and learning on my feet.' After eighteen months, at the age of forty-seven, Dana landed a job as PA to the managing director of the Reading office of an expanding American software company. In the late 1990s, Dana rode the IT boom with her boss, who was rapidly promoted to become a senior vice-president with responsibility for Europe and Latin America. But in 2000 the tech bubble burst, and the company started cutting its workforce. In her self-improving fashion, Dana was willing to spread herself wider in order to fill in the gaps. 'I was actually doing office and facilities management and managing the reception area and all that stuff. Because as companies make cuts you have to take on other roles, and I took them on very willingly and very ably. I liked multi-tasking; it was fun.'

It never occurred to Dana that her own job might be vulnerable. Nor did it occur to her colleagues. 'When you're working for the senior VP of the company, naturally – let's put it this way – lots of people said, "Well, you're alright, Dana."'

Dana only realised that she might be fired in the spring of 2005, when the management circulated an e-mail warning that people in 'unique' positions were liable to have their jobs eliminated. A few days later she was given her notice, after nine years with the company. 'I wasn't bitter, but I was very, very distraught. I guess what happens to you is that you say, "I can't believe it's happening to me." But I think that's normal, isn't it?'

Dana persuaded her former boss to buy a few hours' time for her with a personnel consultant, who offered advice about writing her CV and interview technique. Then she was on her own, with two months' redundancy money in her purse, a 100 per cent mortgage on her small house in Reading and no savings. In the following weeks, she trawled the internet hunting for suitable PA positions, and eventually found one advertised with a local employment agency. Unfortunately the position had already been filled, but the agency persuaded her to take a contract position as a PA for another American technology multinational with a major European division in Reading.

> From that moment on I was the most miserable woman on earth. I hated every minute of it. You're a contractor, so there's absolutely no commitment to you, understandably. But I'm a loyal person who likes to give and receive commitment, so it felt very alien. Everybody worked remotely, on a hot desk with their laptop and mobile phone. It was just horrid.

Dana decided to grit her teeth and carry on, because she badly needed the money. For the next eight months she searched for other jobs with no luck, despite having several interviews. Finally in January 2006, two weeks after her contract ended, she was hired as an office manager with a small recruitment agency in Reading. She was happier here, but still frustrated that a lot of the work was simply monitoring office processes such as payroll administration, rather than taking decisions. Dana carried on networking, and in April 2006 she was headhunted for a position as PA to the chief executive, chief financial officer and marketing director of Xafinity, a business software outsourcing company based in Reading.

Dana is convinced this is the right job for her, but after

experiencing redundancy once, she is taking nothing for granted:

> You never know what companies are going to do. You don't know what the future will hold, whether your CEO might want to move on, and whether whoever moves in might say, 'Oh no, I don't want to take over that person.' So staying would be good, moving up would be brilliant, but I haven't too many high expectations. Not now. I've got to be realistic.

*

As Dana and Ian have learnt from hard experience, modern corporate culture is a world away from the steady certainties of the Three Bs era. In Reading, as elsewhere, people over fifty have to absorb several crucial home truths for older people in the modern labour market. For a start, there is no point believing that modern companies have any interest in managing employees' careers over a projected 40–45-year time span (see Box 2.3). Most businesses take a much shorter-term view of the employer–employee relationship.

Box 2.3: Anthony – coping with corporate upheaval

Every day, Anthony turns up for work as a senior IT analyst at a telecoms company in Reading, unsure whether he will still be in a job by the evening. His firm nearly went out of business during the 2000–1 technology slump, and still faces a highly uncertain future following a merger with a rival group. 'There has been a big turnover. I've had eight different bosses in the last eighteen months. Had I not already been working here, would I have got a job in the newly structured company? I think it's highly unlikely.'

Aged fifty-nine, Anthony has an annual base salary of

£60,000. With more than thirty years' experience in the industry, he is confident that he could find work if he ever lost his job. Yet he laments the passing of a more compassionate management culture: 'In the old, more paternalistic [information technology] industry, when a good manager's department ceased to exist, he or she would make sure that all their people were redeployed in useful jobs elsewhere in the company, and he would trust his manager to do the same thing. Twice in my career that has happened. I built up a department from nothing to forty-five people in three years, and then we sold this business, so suddenly the department had no need to exist any more. I found new jobs for all my people, and my boss found a new job for me. The same thing happened a few years later.'

In sharp contrast, when a job is axed by Anthony's current employer, the redundant employee is almost always shown the door. From Anthony's perspective, that means his first loyalty these days is to himself. 'Each time there is a cutback, you feel like it's the angel of death sweeping over the company, and you wonder who is going to get cut out this time. So you don't have this confidence that you're going to be with the same company for forty years. Perhaps that's good.'

The new HR model is firmly implanted at Thames Valley Park, a verdant business estate that was created in the late 1980s on a riverside site near the old Suttons Seeds plantation grounds. In the past fifteen years, the park has attracted a cluster of multinationals, including Microsoft and Oracle (both of which have their European headquarters in Reading) and BG, the gas exploration group. Employment conditions in the park are a world away from the monotonous factory routines of the Three Bs era. Ducks waddle across the riverside campus, while inside the park's glass and steel office blocks, squadrons of self-styled 'knowledge workers' hot-desk with their laptops around airy open-plan spaces.

This shifting, transient scene is reflected in the personnel policies of many of the companies located in the park. At BG, Mike Thomas, the group's 56-year-old pensions manager, sums up the new thinking:

I think the philosophy has changed. When I did my actuarial training many years ago it was an era when you had a job for life, and you were looking at a two-thirds pension on your final salary, and what mattered in plan design was income replacement ratios. Companies projected that. They said, 'If this employee stays with us we want to make sure he's got a decent standard of living when he retires,' and that was how final-salary schemes came about.

Today, people [often] stay in jobs for just five years, and the focus is much more on how much this employee is costing us for the five years that he is working for us. We're going to give him his salary . . . and we're going to give him some money that he can put towards retirement. But companies have no responsibility for how that person is going to fare years down the road, by which time they may have had half a dozen other jobs.

Thames Valley Park is also striking for its youthful ambience. An older jobseeker applying for a vacancy here could easily be dispirited, because most of the workers are in the 20–45 age group. Dhana Markanday, the permanent jobs manager at the Reed Employment agency in Reading, which does a lot of placement work on the park, confirms that ageism is a fact of life in the town's new economy:

Reed Employment's remit is that we work on all types of people regardless of gender, race or age. We actively work on that premise. However, on the flip side of the coin, you sometimes find clients who will look very closely at a CV and say, 'Well, we don't want people who are that experienced.' And what that means is, 'We don't think they'll fit in because of their age.'

Markanday does not agree with this attitude, but she has some sympathy as well.

It's difficult for the clients, because if you've got a marketing department that's full of 22-year-olds, and then suddenly a 50-year-old with twenty years' experience of marketing wants to downsize and become a marketing administrator, that means the whole company culture has to change. How we tend to educate the clients is to say, 'For goodness sake, you're getting a bargain. At the end of the day, you've got somebody there with twenty years' background who doesn't want to be a marketing manager any more and just wants to come in, do their job and go home.' Sometimes it works, and sometimes it doesn't.

But Markanday also says that older people can be their own worst enemies when trying to overcome such attitudes, because they often meekly accept ageist stereotypes about the alleged unsuitability of certain jobs and sectors for anyone over fifty. She cites the experience of one of her clients at Thames Valley Park, ING Direct, the internet and telephone bank that is owned by ING, the Dutch financial services multinational. In 2004, ING Direct began a recruitment drive in the Reading area, prior to the launch of its British operation. Many of these positions were for call centre work. Lindsay Sinclair, ING Direct's UK chief executive, explains that the bank's attempts to hire across a wide age range proved problematic: 'We found we were attracting very many young people and we made a greater effort to try to reach out to advertise to older people, because they bring experience and maturity. When calls are flying thick and fast . . . they sort of provide a cool head.'

ING decided to target some of its recruitment advertising at local newspapers in the Reading area, which market research suggested would be more effective in attracting applications from older people. Yet the response rate was still disappointing, as the age profile of the workforce in the summer of 2005 illustrated. By then, ING had more than 500 full-time and part-time employees at Thames Valley Park, but only about 6 per cent were over the age of fifty. The bank has continued to encourage older people to apply for vacancies, with little success, according to Markanday:

> They actively look for CVs of [older] people, and they just don't get them. It could be because people of that generation don't want a call centre job, or it could be because they don't even try to go for it, because they think, 'Well, there's no way I'm going to get an interview.'

It is a similar picture at Yell, the business directories group, whose head office overlooks Reading's noisy Inner Distribution Road. In the summer of 2005, only twelve members of Yell's total British payroll of 3,500 were aged over sixty, and only 264 were between the ages of fifty and fifty-nine. Simon Gale, the group's HR director, says the main reason for the dearth of older people is simply because they do not apply for vacancies, most of which are in Yell's hard-driving sales division.

> Within Yell, a lot of work is highly energised. It requires a lot of this daily effort where you've got to get up every morning and go and see a customer and be as bright and cheerful and presentable with the last customer of the week as you would be with the first one. But it

doesn't end there. It goes on day after day, week after week, and year after year. Because our pay schemes in the sales area are performance oriented, there's a suggestion, I think, being very simplistic and generalistic about it, that it's more of a young person's domain.

Gale stresses that this is not his opinion. But it is easy to see how such a mindset can be mutually reinforced, as a shortage of older applicants for 'dynamic' jobs strengthens management's belief that some positions are not suited to the fifty-plus age group.

It is, indeed, self-defeating for jobseekers in their fifties or older to reduce their employment prospects by ruling out whole sections of the labour market. The onus is on them to adapt to the demands of businesses that hire workers in order to increase profits. This point is repeatedly emphasised by front-line employment experts such as Markanday and Jean Charmak, the head of the Forest recruitment agency in Reading, as well as job counsellors such as Sue Culver at the Reading TEA Shop. But it is a fact of capitalist life that is sometimes overlooked by age campaigners who talk optimistically about how companies will have to fit jobs around the needs of older people in the greyer workplace of the future. In reality, no company will ever go down this route unless it suits their operating model.

How can an older person sustain his or her career in the new world of work? Beyond an indispensable strength of character, they need to be able to keep pace with accelerating economic changes in order to have any chance of finding and keeping a job. In Reading – a thriving town in the most prosperous region of the world's fourth largest economy – those changes are part of a wider transformation of western Europe and North America. Three features in particular define Reading's modern economy: a shift from manufacturing to retail and services; increasing globalisation; and an increasing emphasis on skills, even in traditionally low-grade occupations.

Anyone in the fifty-plus age group who can adapt to these trends has a reasonable prospect of sustaining a successful career. But as the chapters which follow illustrate, Reading's employers are usually not in the business of handing out route maps to older jobseekers who have lost their bearings.

3   Shopping for jobs

Brian Carter is arguably the most age-friendly employer in Reading. He is the managing director of Jacksons department store, self-styled 'outfitters of distinction', which has been selling womenswear, school uniforms and haberdashery since 1875 from the same corner of Duke Street in the town centre (known universally as Jacksons Corner). Carter – who is descended on his mother's side from the founding Jackson family – refuses to divulge his age, but says he started at the store in 1963. So far, he has turned a deaf ear to his wife's suggestion that he might eventually consider retiring. With a glance at the ancestral portraits on his office wall, he blames the example set by his predecessors. 'My grandfather kept going two to three days a week till he was seventy-nine. His brother kept on till he was eighty-four. My uncle, Edward Jackson, had bone cancer, and died at seventy-four. But he didn't retire, he just couldn't get here.'

The Jacksons' 'work till you drop' ethos is instilled in the store's payroll of full-time and part-time staff, approximately eighty strong, of whom about two-thirds are women. Carter reckons that almost half his employees do not pay national insurance contributions because they are over the state pension age.

At times you just have to give them a hint that maybe they should cut down a little more. Sometimes it's a bit embarrassing, but generally we don't get rid of anyone here because of their age. Generally, they want to cut down their hours because when they're taking a pension they don't want to pay too much tax on their salary . . . [But] if they're five minutes late for work, they're terribly upset. Whereas the younger ones think, well, the hell with it.

It is tempting to portray Jacksons as a latter-day version of Grace Brothers, the antiquated family-owned department store that featured in the 1970s television comedy series *Are You Being Served?*. Cash and receipts at Jacksons are still despatched in specially designed steel canisters that shoot around the labyrinthine building through a complex internal network of pneumatic tubes. The droll, dapper Carter proudly notes that it is the last such system still in operation in a British shop. And as he looks down on Duke Street from his cramped office, he seems loftily detached from the retail explosion that has erupted around Jacksons Corner over the past three decades.

A short distance away, the glitzy Oracle shopping centre – opened in 1999 on a riverside site close to the old Courage brewery – has capitalised on south-east England's consumer boom to become one of the region's biggest retail emporiums. Local Reading retailers such as Wellsteeds, a rival department store to Jacksons, have long since disappeared from Broad Street, the town's main shopping thorough-fare, which is now dominated by major high street brands. Around Reading, Tesco, Sainsbury's, Asda and Morrisons (formerly Safeway) have all opened hypermarkets since the 1980s that have decimated the local grocery trade.

This influx may have been bad news for many old-style Reading retailers, but it has transformed the town's labour market. Retail dis-tribution and consumer services (including hotels and restaurants) account for 26 per cent of all jobs in Reading, with almost 26,000 people employed in the sector in 2004. Meanwhile, less than 5 per cent of all local jobs are in manufacturing, once a mainstay of Reading's economy.* Carter remains unmoved by all this competition: 'It hasn't made a lot of difference, to be honest. We were a bit concerned about what was going to happen, but I think a lot of our customers went in there [to the new shops] and thought, "Well, they're not really catering for me."'

The irony is that Jacksons has the same personnel management model as the other retail heavyweights that have come to Reading in force. Both Jacksons and its more famous national competitors depend on older people to fill a range of shop floor positions. For example, in the summer of 2005 almost a quarter of John Lewis's 881 staff at its Reading department store on Broad Street were over the age of fifty. The pay is low for most of these customer service jobs, as is demonstrated by the wage rates at Sainsbury's hypermarket in Calcot on the western outskirts of Reading. In 2005, a full-time 'colleague' at the Calcot store immediately below supervisor level received £5.19 per hour, plus a 'London weighting' of 45p per hour, for a 39-hour week, amounting to a basic annual salary (not including overtime) of £11,438.

Nonetheless, many older people in Reading work in such low-grade retail jobs primarily for the money. Janice is typical of this breed. Now in her 'late fifties', she has worked in various shop floor jobs at Sainsbury's Calcot store over the past twenty years. Janice always saw her pay as for 'treats and things' until her husband was unexpectedly made redundant from his factory job in 2003. Her husband is still out of work, and Janice has other financial worries. When she first joined Sainsbury's, she was 'badly advised' and decided to take out a private pension rather than enrol in the company's plan. Having failed to pay sufficient additional voluntary

*Labour Market Survey: Reading (Durham: Nomis, 2005).

contributions, she fears her pension will be much less than she was expecting. As a result of these mishaps, Janice has been forced to reassess her career at Sainsbury's.

I always said I would retire at sixty, but the way things are going it makes you think twice, because of pensions and the cost of things. And I think as you do get nearer that age when you are perhaps considering retirement, you're thinking, what will I do without that kind of money?

Beyond money, many older people in Reading are attracted to this kind of retail work because – like Pete Dunne at B&Q (see Chapter 2) – they enjoy the social side of the job. Anne McCurry, a seventy-year-old cashier at John Lewis's Reading branch, originally retired at the age of sixty-two, after seventeen years with the store, with a reasonable company pension. But a year later she asked to come back as a part-time cashier, working three days a week in the electrical department, even though she did not need the money.

I suppose there are two or three reasons for working. I've been on my own for quite a while. I found in that year I had out, although I was OK, and I had lots of things to do, there is only so much dusting and things that you *can* do. And sometimes, it's not always the work that you miss, it's the company and the atmosphere – the buzz of getting up and knowing I've got to do something definite.

Jim Armstrong is another pensioner who has taken a part-time retail job to get out of the home. Every weekday morning, this lanky 75-year-old former building company manager strides up and down the aisles at Asda's Reading superstore with a handheld microphone, announcing special offers and directing shoppers who need help to the customer services desk. Jim – who is originally from Glasgow – seems born for the role of store 'greeter'. He is immaculately turned out in a green Asda blazer and pressed grey flannels, and keeps up a tireless stream of folksy patter as he welcomes shoppers into the store. But as he explains, the job's real purpose from his point of view is to smooth relations on the domestic front. 'I retired when I was sixty-five and my wife and me had a chat. She chatted and I listened, as one does. And it was agreed that she didn't want me under her feet 24/7, and I could see her point.'

Jim has a well-funded personal pension and some modest investments, so he is not bothered by Asda's low pay scale, which for this kind of job is not much higher than the national minimum wage. 'Let's be quite honest about it; I don't come here for the money. My wife is Irish, and she's very volatile. And I'm not. So she gets time to do her own thing.'

Big retailers such as B&Q, Asda and Sainsbury's point to the droves of visible older shop floor staff on their payroll like Jim, Anne and Janice as evidence that they are in the vanguard of efforts to break down ageism in the workplace. And in Reading, as elsewhere in Britain, there is no doubt that the big retail chains chase older workers aggressively. Kevin Oram, the energetic young personnel manager at Reading's Tesco Extra hypermarket, is so keen to hire older people (and indeed, people of all ages) that he regularly tries to lure them away from rival retailers.

> I go out and headhunt. So I will go into other outlets, like B&Q, Sainsbury's, wherever, and I will actively look for talent. Go on spec, with my business cards, and shake hands, say, 'I like what I've seen today,' and ask if they're interested in a change of career. Sainsbury's and others do it. That's fine. If we don't treat our staff well, then the competition will poach them.

Oram is equally determined to retain older Tesco employees in the Reading area who are approaching the state pension age. 'My job is to encourage people to work beyond the state retirement age, because I don't want to lose that talent.'

To help keep them on his books, Oram receives regular reports from Tesco's national database in Cardiff about which employees in the Reading region (an area that also covers parts of Hampshire and Surrey) have less than six months before they are eligible for the state pension. He then tries to persuade them to carry on at Tesco, either on a full-time or a part-time basis.

Recruiting sergeants such as Oram provide the human numbers that allow the major national retailers to burnish their anti-ageist credentials. Asda, a subsidiary of Wal-Mart, the American retail multinational, claimed in 2005 to be Britain's biggest employer of older people, with more than 25,000 staff over the age of fifty. In its accompanying press release, Asda explained why it targeted this age group for shop floor vacancies: 'Asda knew that over-fifties were more than capable of making as big a contribution to the workplace as people less than half their age and had found that their wealth of experience made them particularly good choices for customer-facing roles such as people greeters or customer service colleagues.'

Not to be outdone, Sainsbury's announced in the spring of 2005 that it was hoping to recruit 10,000 people above the age of fifty, principally to boost staffing levels behind delicatessen counters during the busy Christmas season. Justin King, Sainsbury's chief executive (who was forty-four at the time), used a homely illustration to demonstrate why older people made excellent supermarket employees: 'Their life experience means that they know the softer side of customer service, such as how to carve a lamb joint. I don't know how to do it, because every time I go home my dad carves the meat. He won't let me near the carving board.' King warmed to his theme on Sainsbury's careers website, where the company launched a recruitment drive in 2005 called 'Generation 50+':

> Our customers tell us that they value our colleagues being able to talk to them on their level. Many of our customers are older, but interestingly even our younger customers tell us that they value the experience that older colleagues can give them. An ability to be able to talk while sitting on the till about what's going on in their lives. A little bit of extra knowledge about meat or fish if they're working on a counter. Or just an overall ability to engage with them, which all of us get greater experience with, the older we get.

Such statements from the top of the retail industry reflect the received wisdom at shop floor level about the benefits of employing older people – views that are shared by managers in other customer service industries (see Box 3.1).

Box 3.1: Dial 50+ for room service

Stephanie Norman, human resources and training manager at the Millennium Madejski Hotel in Reading, echoes her counterparts in the retail sector when she extols the merits of older staff over younger employees. 'The difference we find as the employer is that if we have somebody who is slightly more mature, that's what you get as well. They are more mature, they have got a bit of life experience. If the guests complain, they know why. Whereas if you have a school leaver who deals with a problem, it's very much a Kevin the Teenager syndrome. They shrug their shoulders and don't understand. They have no empathy.'

Mark Valiant, manager of the House of Fraser department store in Reading's Oracle shopping centre, is emphatic about the value of older staff. He identifies formal wear, cosmetics and lighting as sections where he is particularly keen to place them: 'Obviously if you've got a maturer woman who has been used to using the products, then people naturally trust their judgement. Whereas with a seventeen-year-old girl who has no experience, all she can really do is read the back of the box.' To illustrate his point further, Valiant calls over Mike Lancaster, a spry, 65-year-old retail veteran whom he has recently hired to work in the lighting department. Mike's last job was managing a luggage shop on London's Edgware Road. In April 2004 the lease on the shop expired and he was made redundant. Mike, who is divorced, moved back to Reading, where his recently deceased twin brother had left him a flat. He spent six months doing up the property, and then wondered what to do next, given that he had enough savings from various investments not to need to work.

I got totally bored out of my mind, having worked from the age of eighteen. I literally drove round the countryside that I hadn't seen for God knows how many years and I thought, 'Well, I can't do this for the next year. I've got to find a job.' So I then applied to virtually every company in Reading in the retail trade.

Mike ended up at House of Fraser because, as he puts it, the store wanted someone 'with a lot of retail selling experience' to work full time in the lighting department. He took the job, even though he had been originally looking for a part-time vacancy.

One can see why a store manager would want to hire Mike. He is friendly, intelligent, and obviously knowledgeable about the products he is required to sell. Yet Mike and thousands of other older staff who serve customers in Reading's shopping malls, supermarkets and retail warehouses are not proof in themselves that the retail sector is thoroughly age friendly. For a start, labelling employees in the fifty-plus age group as more mature than their younger colleagues is a clear breach of the new age discrimination law.* Philip Taylor, founder of the Cambridge Research Centre on Ageing, says that Sainsbury's in particular fell into an ageist trap of its own making when Justin King launched the 'Generation 50+' campaign:

> Sainsbury's were saying that younger workers were not as competent as older workers, which was age stereotyping in extremis. It was using one set of age stereotypes to challenge another, as if older workers are now better than other workers, and younger workers are just layabouts who stay in bed and have got no Protestant work ethic at all.

Sainsbury's withdrew the Generation 50+ link from its online recruitment site shortly before the age law came into force in October 2006.

Beyond the legal difficulties raised by this style of recruitment, the claim by leading retailers to an age-friendly moral high ground is undermined from two directions. First, the attraction of older staff to these companies rests to a large degree on the willingness of many of them who do not have extensive child care or family commitments to work unsocial hours in the evenings and at weekends, when Britain does most of its shopping. In this regard, the claim by retail chains to fit jobs around older people's lifestyles is bogus; it is older people's lifestyles that suit these companies' business model. The same business model makes it easy for retail groups such as B&Q and Sainsbury's to offer tailored benefits for older staff, according to Sarah Vickerstaff, Professor of Work and Employment

---

*All the interviews for this book were conducted before the law took effect.

at the University of Kent: 'They [the big national retail companies] almost run 24/7 operations. A vast proportion of their staff are on flexible contracts . . . so offering gradual retirement, "Benidorm leave" and all these other benefits for older workers is not a very big step operationally, because they're used to managing complex rotas and systems.'

There is nothing wrong with providing low-paid, flexible work to millions of people in the fifty-plus age group who might otherwise be unemployed, even if the underlying business rationale for hiring them is rather more hard headed than retailers sometimes suggest. But there is a second flaw in the anti-ageist case made by many leading retail groups: when they make the case, they are usually only referring to the shop floor. Further up the corporate hierarchy, retail management remains primarily a younger person's game.

The age profile of Sainsbury's workforce at its Calcot store is typical of the industry. In June 2005, the store employed 655 people, of whom 626 were defined as 'colleagues' (meaning shop floor staff) and twenty-nine were defined as managers. In total, 320 full-time and part-time personnel were over the age of forty-five. But there was a marked difference between the proportion of 'colleagues' in this age group (50 per cent) and the proportion of managers (27 per cent).

This kind of age imbalance between shop floor staff and management extends right to the top of the industry. Consider the example set by Britain's three leading supermarket groups. Tesco, Britain's biggest retailer, says that about 20 per cent of its workforce nationally is over the age of fifty. But in September 2006, the company's fifty-year-old CEO, Sir Terry Leahy, was the only one of six senior executives on the main board who scraped into this employee age group. The other five were all in their mid- to late forties. It was a similar story at Sainsbury's, where the chairman, chief executive and chief financial officer were respectively 52, 44 and 39. At Asda, Andy Bond, the group's 42-year-old CEO, headed a senior management team that was mostly composed of people in their thirties and forties.

It is a safe bet that a large proportion of these highly paid executives will have retired from their present jobs well before they reach their sixties. Stephen McNair, director of the Centre for Research into the Older Workforce, recalls visiting one leading retailer which was proud of its record on age issues: 'They said, "Yes, we have this wonderful [anti-ageist] policy. Our oldest employee is eighty-seven." And when we said, "Does that apply to all levels of staff?" they said, "It doesn't apply to senior managers, because the pension scheme is so attractive that they're all gone by fifty-two."'

This early-retirement culture filters a long way down the management ranks at some large retail groups. Danny O'Sullivan, the 38-year-old manager of B&Q's Reading branch, works for a company that has built a reputation as one of Britain's most welcoming employers for older people. Dressed in B&Q's trademark orange apron, O'Sullivan subscribes enthusiastically to the retail industry line about the advantages of employing the fifty-plus generation in customer service roles. 'From a commercial standpoint, the guys we have over the age of fifty who've had experience in home improvement have got such a wealth of knowledge . . . There's also the piece which says because of their life experience, they're mature people anyway.' However, O'Sullivan does not himself intend to still be working full time at this age. 'I'd like to retire in my mid-fifties. B&Q is a good business that pays quite well, and I'm in a pretty fortunate position in terms of cash.'

None of this means that retail groups are overtly hostile to older people in management roles. At Sainsbury's Calcot store, Anne Murch (see Chapter 1), the 69-year-old deputy petrol station manager, is one of a number of 'colleagues' in the fifty-plus age group whose skills and experience have been deemed too valuable to waste on basic till or shelf-stacking work (see Box 3.2). Yet the suspicion remains that any dedicated retail executive looking to sustain his or her career beyond the age of sixty will be rowing against powerful corporate currents.

Box 3.2: Peter Johnson – the determined downsizer

Peter Johnson's odyssey from nuclear weapons to supermarket work began in 2002. At the age of fifty-two, Peter took voluntary redundancy from his job as a facilities engineer at the Atomic Weapons Establishment in Aldermaston, near Reading. After thirty-two years' service, Peter walked away with an annual net income of more than £12,000 and the vague idea that he would potter around his garden while his wife continued to work at Aldermaston as an administrator. For a few months he was content. 'But when it came to the end of the year, about October, and we got the darker evenings and the damp weather, it got a bit boring. So I started looking for a part-time job.'

Peter initially wanted to stay in engineering, but he quickly ran into age prejudice. 'With two or three of the jobs that I did get interviews for, I was told that I was overqualified. They said, "We'd take you on, but with your qualifications you can get a better job, so you're not looking to stay with the company." So I said, "I'm not looking for a better job." On at least a couple of occasions, I was told by the person who interviewed me that I had more qualifications than they did. I think there might have been a bit of suspicion on their part that I might come in and take their job. I can't say I resented it, but I found it a bit disappointing because that wasn't my intention.'

With no financial worries, Peter decided to take an unpaid, voluntary job, driving pensioners in a minibus to Sainsbury's Calcot store. On one of these trips, he saw a vacancy for a part-time shelf-stacking job and decided to apply. 'Basically, I think you could call it [a desire for] the quiet life. I didn't have to worry if I was stacking Heinz soup today, baked beans tomorrow, no problems . . . I was just looking for something low key, more to occupy me than to earn a living.'

Sainsbury's, however, had other ideas. 'I came in for an interview with the personnel manager, who said, "We've looked through your records, and we think you'd be wasted with your experience. You're a professional engineer and a health and safety officer. We think we could use you, and you could help us."' Peter was hired as the store's part-time health and safety officer, with additional responsibility for building and equipment maintenance. In terms of the job description, it is the same role that he had at Aldermaston. The main difference is that Sainsbury's does not make nuclear warheads.

Peter Wanless testifies to the effort involved. Originally from the north-east, Peter is a hard-driving retail operations executive who has worked in the industry since leaving school in 1965. He moved to Reading in 1984 when he left his previous employer, Asda, to become a department manager at Sainsburys' Calcot store. In 1999, Peter was promoted to a middle management job at the group's head office in London, where he helped to organise Sainsbury's non-food operations. Five years later, at the age of fifty-six, he accepted a voluntary redundancy package. 'My father was very ill, and my mother had just died, and my son had just started a business. Really, I'd been working so many hours for so long there was a whole host of things which it was just nice to catch up with.'

Peter also reckoned that this was the right time financially to leave Sainsbury's.

A couple of things swung it for me. One was my concern about the pension thing, in that if they had been acquired by another foreign company, there was quite a big deficit in the pension fund and there was always the possibility that I could lose out . . . At that time, I was three and a half years away from retirement. I had the option [under the voluntary redundancy package] to contribute an amount into the pension fund which would actually minimise – say, by about half – the loss in pension because I was leaving early.

Peter never intended to retire permanently, even though his package was generous. In total, he came away with a lump sump of about £36,000 after tax, plus a reduced Sainsbury's pension entitlement when he reached the age of sixty. It was a good deal, but in April 2005, he started to job-hunt in earnest. As someone who had worked all his life, he was feeling restless. His financial situation was also quite tight, because he had used his severance cheque to pay off the mortgage on his house, and his wife was now being threatened with redundancy from her job as a cashier at the Reading office of the Department for Work and Pensions.

This was the start of his difficulties. When we first met, Peter had been applying in vain for senior retail management vacancies for over six months, and his frustration was palpable. He was convinced that his age was proving a critical handicap.

The only authority I had at Sainsbury's was the fact, really, that I was hardly ever wrong. I'd just seen it all. Now that's a lot of experience and judgement to take to another company. However, it became apparent that these [retail] companies weren't going to take the bait, and so I started applying for jobs I knew I could do quite easily, like [supermarket] night shift manager, because they're still paying about £35,000. And the management recruitment agencies hardly got any response to anything I sent in. So I rang them up and said, 'What's going on?' And they said, 'You're just too old. [They] won't entertain you.'

Peter pressed one of the recruitment agencies about why the retail firms allegedly took this view.

I was told that they don't see you've got all the qualifications to do this job. They'd rather get somebody who was younger. I was also told that retail is a tough environment. I said, 'Well, I know that, I've been in it all my life.' They said, 'It's long hours.' I said, 'I know that, I've been used to working about sixty to seventy hours a week, every week.

Peter eventually asked to speak to a senior consultant at another recruitment agency where he was registered.

I said, 'Why am I not getting anywhere?' And he said, 'I'll just check your CV and I'll ring you back,' which he did. And he said, 'It's not what you want to hear, but basically you're too old . . . They will all say they are not ageist, but the reality is that they are. You're wasting your time . . . It's not good for you; give up, go and do something else.'

Peter took the recruiter's advice. In the autumn of 2005, he obtained a provisional heavy goods vehicle (HGV) driver's licence, while continuing to apply for retail management jobs. His plan was to take a training course, at a cost of about £1,000, and become a fully qualified lorry driver. Peter's reasoning was simple: as a truck driver, his age would not be such a disadvantage.

There's currently about 80,000 vacancies for HGV drivers in the UK. Most [employers] won't take drivers under twenty-five because of the insurance. A lot of the drivers now are older people who are retiring. There's virtually no training in the industry because drivers move around from company to company . . . I'm sure that once you get your licence and you get some experience, looking forward you're really not going to be out of a job.

His hunch proved correct. In January 2006, Peter started a lorry-driving job delivering newspapers and magazines for W. H. Smith. Ironically, it was at this point that his luck finally changed on the retail job-hunting front. In February 2006, he successfully applied for a position as a store manager in Reading for Dunelm Mill, a home furnishing retail chain which had just opened a superstore on the same Calcot trading estate as Sainsbury's. After a disquieting brush with the world of long-term unemployment, Peter was back where he had begun in Reading.

*

Peter Wanless's story does not prove in itself that ageism is rife above shop floor level in the retail industry. As he says, he is only reporting what he was told by various recruitment agencies about why he could not get a job.

What his experience certainly demonstrates is the competitiveness of the modern retail trade, compared with the days when the shopping scene in Reading and other similar towns was dominated by local family stores such as Jacksons and Wellsteeds. This is the main challenge for older people looking to sustain a career in the industry above the shop floor, regardless of whether further obstacles are then thrown in their path by ageist employers. And it is a challenge that extends across the entire modern services sector, from banks and insurers to hotels, shops and restaurants (see Box 3.3).

Box 3.3: Maurice – the insurance clerk who failed to insure his career

In 1996, Maurice resigned from his job as a commercial clerk in the Reading branch of a large British insurance firm in order to get treatment for his asthma. He has been out of work ever since. Today, this mild-mannered 57-year-old bachelor sits in the small Reading flat he must sell to repair his finances, amid a pile of packing cases and the ruins of his career.

Maurice mostly blames his ill health and ageist attitudes in the insurance industry for his problems. He did not feel well enough to start job-hunting in earnest until 2004, by which time he had run through most of his savings. And when he started to phone local insurance firms, he found his age was a disadvantage. 'When I rang up this broker to talk to him, I overheard the conversation between the secretary and this guy. The girl was saying, "He sounds like a good one. He's been in insurance for thirty years." And he said, "Well, if he's been in insurance for thirty years, he's probably too old for us."'

But Maurice has also failed to keep up with developments in the industry. He is a fellow of the Chartered Insurance Institute (CII), but glances ruefully at the unopened professional casebooks that he has ordered from the CII to make himself employable. 'In fairness to everybody, part of the problem with me is that I've been out of insurance for so long.'

Maurice may never work again, not because of prejudice about his age, but because in a more competitive era he has nothing to sell a prospective employer. In the mid-1990s there were still plenty of Maurices occupying fairly safe berths in staid insurance businesses. Today most of these plodders have been weeded out during the industry's relentless consolidation. Maurice's old firm is a case in point. In the past decade it has merged with a British competitor which in turn has been taken over by one of the world's largest insurance groups.

As he prepares to move to an even smaller, rented flat, Maurice senses his career is over. 'I have been through times of

being very worried. You just feel like there's a great chasm
opening up under you and you think, "What am I going to do?"' '

There is a local dimension to this ever-increasing competition. In
Reading, it has Brian Carter keeping an eye on John Lewis or Marks
& Spencer, just a five-minute walk from Jacksons Corner, even as he
retains an imperturbable air. But this local rivalry (replicated by
other retail providers such as banks and hotels) connects with a
global economy which barely impinged on places like Reading a
generation ago. It is not simply that much of Jacksons' womenswear
range is now made in China; or that the tills at Asda's hypermarket
in the Reading suburb of Lower Earley are ultimately connected to
Wal-Mart's back office in Bentonville, Arkansas; or that the Abbey
branch on Broad Street is owned by Spain's Banco Santander. In
addition, many of the non-manufacturing businesses that have put
down roots in Reading since the 1980s serve markets that are literally
borderless. This globalisation – and its impact on the older workforce – is the subject of the following chapter.

4   The high-tech age barrier

From the outside, Comtek is indistinguishable from the small commercial printers and car repair firms that inhabit a shabby trading estate in Reading. The company occupies a yellow and grey prefabricated office block, next to a stationery label producer. Yet Comtek's business is a world away from its neighbours. Founded in 1989 by Askar Shebani, an Iranian exile with a degree in electronic engineering, it installs and maintains computer systems for corporate clients around the world. Shebani – who still owns and runs Comtek – has a worldwide staff of 120 engineers, annual sales of £20 million, and branches in Reading, north Wales, Amsterdam, Frankfurt and California.

Comtek is a minor player in an information technology revolution that has connected Reading to the global economy over the past two decades. Shebani's business is an oddity not because it was started in his garden shed (such founding myths are commonplace in Reading's teeming IT sector), but because its nondescript head office looks and feels like one of the local manufacturers that used to dominate the town's economy. By contrast, most of the sleek technology and telecoms firms in the IT parks that encircle Reading could have been transplanted from Silicon Valley. For it is Reading's similarity with other IT hubs around the world – in particular, its strategic location and well-educated workforce –

which explains its appeal to technology giants such as Oracle, Microsoft, and Hewlett-Packard, all of which have substantial operations in the town.

The official labour market statistics do not show how many people work in Reading's technology and telecoms sector. But according to the borough council, five of the ten largest local private sector employers are high-tech multinationals. Thousands more people work for smaller IT firms that cluster around these giants. Reading thus offers a glimpse of the globalised, post-industrial future envisaged by European leaders at the Lisbon summit in March 2000. They agreed on a series of targets which, if achieved, would transform the EU into 'the most dynamic and competitive knowledge-based economy in the world' by 2010. In this vision, information technology would not only accelerate the advent of a single European market; it would also overhaul lumbering, inefficient companies across all sectors, so they could take on competitors anywhere in the world. It was, in short, a blueprint for a future made for the smart young people with their laptops and lattes who work in high-tech centres such as Reading.

But is it a future that holds any welcome for the fifty-plus age group, many of whom want to extend their careers well beyond the – admittedly unrealistic – 2010 deadline for realising the Lisbon agenda? After all, the IT sector's track record on age issues is about as bad as it gets. During the dot-com craze of the late 1990s the industry made a fetish of youth, hailing a wave of twenty-something internet entrepreneurs as business geniuses, shortly before they went out of business. Even worse, much of the industry operated on a default setting which deleted anyone over forty from future manpower planning, on the grounds that he or she could not possibly keep abreast of technological change.

Sitting in his sparsely furnished office at Comtek, the 53-year-old

Shebani declares such idiocies a thing of the past. 'It used to be like that, but I think a lot of [technology] companies find there is more stability in people above thirty-five.' Shebani says that the average age of his twenty-five Reading-based employees is the 'mid-forties', and that one of his senior engineers is sixty-four. 'Normally, the retirement age is sixty-five, but if an employee wants to carry on working, either part time or full time, I don't really have any objection to it. It depends on their position and circumstances, and the business's need.'

Shebani's views on the subject are echoed by human resources managers at much larger IT companies in Reading. At Oracle (a direct competitor of Comtek), the European division follows the example set by the Californian parent company in having no set retirement age (see Box 4.1). Nick Foster, Oracle's personnel director in Europe, also argues that the industry's attitude towards older people has moved on since the 1990s, as a result of a fundamental change in the way IT products are marketed:

> In the 1980s and 1990s it was a technology sell, so you wanted young people because – rightly or wrongly – they were perceived as being on top of the technology. Now it's all about selling a business solution to businesspeople who have a critical business problem they want to fix. You're typically selling to older, more experienced general managers rather than young, enthusiastic technical specialists, and they want to deal with 'silverbacks'. If you've got a 'silverback' coming in who clearly understands their business situation, you're far more credible as an organisation.

Box 4.1: Peter Dawson – rescued by the age discrimination law

Some IT companies have taken time to catch up with the desire of increasing numbers of older employees to extend their careers. Until 2005, Xansa, a British outsourcing and technology group with headquarters in Reading, had a mandatory retirement age of sixty. That was a serious problem for Peter Dawson, a senior business consultant at Xansa, who was fifty-nine in 2005. A brisk, vigorous Yorkshireman, Peter saw no reason why he should be forced to stop working in his prime. 'I feel that the way the different age groups in companies are dealt with tends to be very cut and dried. You're sixty, cheerio.'

Peter was especially anxious about retiring at sixty because his job-hopping career had prevented him from building up an adequate pension. 'I haven't worked for any organisation for more than twelve years in my working life. During that time I had three or four years where I worked on my own with no pension. Other than that, all the employers I've worked for have provided me with some kind of pension arrangement, and I guess I'm probably going to do better than a lot of people. But even so, it's only going to provide me with a pension of approximately half my working wage.'

Fortunately, Peter's story had a happy ending. At the end of 2005, Xansa decided to raise its retirement age to sixty-five, thus bringing the company in line with the forthcoming age legislation. Peter is convinced that Xansa would not have acted without the legal threat, and is grateful for the chance to resolve his pension shortfall. 'This is helpful to me, because I don't have to concern myself about getting alternative employment, and it offers me the chance to improve my pension on retirement. An extra five years' employment will in my case improve my pension by 50 per cent.'

Oracle's next-door neighbour at Thames Valley Park is SGI, a California-based computer graphics design company, which like Oracle and Microsoft has its European headquarters in Reading. Janet Sporle, SGI's regional human resources manager, says that the industry's age profile may in any case be getting older, because of the after-effect of the technology slump in 2000–1: 'You've got less attrition [of employees] because the IT market generally has been quite difficult, so people are tending to stay longer. Also, because we've been cutting heads, we haven't done that much recruitment. The result is a relatively static workforce in IT terms, which has aged.' Now that the sector is recruiting again, Sporle adds a cautionary note:

> We have it in our policies that we don't discriminate on age and I don't consciously do it in interviews. But do we do it subconsciously? As soon as you think of a dynamic salesperson, what would that person look like? In your head, you've still probably got somebody in mind who's in their early thirties. So I think there's still that generic picture of what a dynamic salesperson looks like. That means you have to be quite careful [when recruiting] because it would be quite easy to discriminate. I'm not talking about SGI in particular, but there's still this perception that younger people are better at high tech. We know it's not true.

Sporle is perhaps right to question whether the technology sector has really shed its ageist habits. Another HR manager at a large IT services company in Thames Valley Park explains that the reason why so many employees take early retirement is essentially because they have run out of steam: 'The profile of our workforce means that many of them are quite high earners, and would be looking to not work for any longer than was necessary. There's a lifestyle that goes along with the work, such as often travelling from Monday to Friday, and perhaps people have had enough and don't want to carry on doing it.'

One fact is clear. The age profile of most large technology firms in Reading is strikingly young, despite Sporle's theory that the proportion of older people is gradually increasing. Oracle does not provide specific demographic data about its Reading-based workforce, but the age breakdown of its European and South African staff, who count as one payroll unit, is revealing. In 2005, 76 per cent of these employees, all managed from Reading, were forty-five or younger, 20 per cent were in the 46–55 age group, and only 4 per cent were older than fifty-six.* At SGI, Sporle estimates that the average age of the company's 120 employees in Reading was somewhere between thirty-five and forty in 2005, compared with an age profile that was 'typically late twenties to late thirties' at the end of the 1990s.

Some of these companies (though not SGI) give the impression that the industry's historic bias towards younger people has skewed the definition of what constitutes a balanced employee age profile. For example, in the summer of 2005 the US telecoms group MCI (since taken over by Verizon, a rival US firm) employed about 1,400 staff at its European headquarters in Reading. Steve Bryan, MCI's head of human resources in Britain and Ireland, explained in an e-mail that the company tried to maintain an age-diverse workforce:

We have a mixture of employees in terms of age, each bringing different skills and experiences to the business. I would say that having a balanced workforce in terms of age, gender and background brings competitive advantage over an organisation that is biased heavily to one or a few groups.

*Company information.

Yet the age structure of MCI's Reading payroll looked thoroughly unbalanced: 80 per cent of local employees were forty-three or younger, 17 per cent were in the 44–56 age group, and a mere 3 per cent were fifty-seven or older.*

Such figures lend credence to the view of many older technology workers that the industry is still riven with ageist prejudice. The reality is more complex, judged by the evidence from Reading. There are plenty of executives whose thoughts on age issues have not progressed since the 1990s. One manager at the Reading offices of a large US technology multinational repeated the ludicrous dot-com era cliché that nobody over forty could write software – including, presumably, the chairman of Microsoft. It is also true, as the example of Don shows (see Chapter 1), that any technology worker of any age will fail to find or keep a job if they do not constantly update their IT skills. But at the opposite extreme, there is a place in the globalised, 'knowledge economy' of the future for suitably qualified older IT specialists, precisely because of their superior experience and skills. Their challenge is to prove this point, in a sector still afflicted by the legacy of deeply rooted ageism.

*

Reading's IT labour market is highly competitive. Dozens of vacancies are posted every day on the websites of specialist IT recruitment agencies, but these jobs are only open to people with suitable qualifications. Jean Charmak, the head of the Forest recruitment agency in Reading, says that despite the town's excellent colleges and universities, many local IT companies complain that the education system is not keeping pace with changes in the industry.

*Company information.

The result, according to Charmak, is that many younger people entering the local IT labour market lack the right skills. 'We have been into Reading University and talked to the people who are running the computer courses, because they are not giving them [the students] the education that they need when they come out into the workplace.'

Meanwhile, older technology workers with inferior or outmoded skills struggle to remain employable in a permanent IT revolution. John, a 58-year-old data analyst at the Reading offices of the telecoms company Cable & Wireless, has a CV that reflects the constant change in the industry. During his career he has done a succession of low-grade jobs that have either become obsolete or been outsourced to Asia.

John originally joined Cable & Wireless straight from school, and was trained as an electronic wireman connecting circuit boards. He then worked at ICL, where he assembled computers, and at the Bank of Ireland in Reading, where he spent eight years as a computer operator in the back office. When his job with the bank was eliminated in 1994, it took John fifteen months to find another permanent position. 'I was forty-six when I was made redundant and I always felt that my age, even then, was against me. I wrote about 300 letters during that time I was unemployed and I think I probably got about six replies.'

In 1995 John was hired by Energis, which at that time was a telecoms subsidiary of the utility National Grid. He started as a call monitor, tracking traffic volume and technical faults on customer lines, and has remained on the payroll despite constant turmoil inside the company since the technology crash of 2000–1. Energis almost went bankrupt in 2002 and was bought in 2005 by Cable & Wireless. John now processes orders from corporate customers for telecoms services and checks whether Cable & Wireless has the right equipment to fulfil the contract. He thinks his job is safe, despite a cost-cutting programme. But he feels insecure, because his disjointed career has left him with a worrying pensions shortfall.

> It's very scary . . . and this is what really annoys me about the government. They say, 'Let's have everybody working till they are seventy.' Who is going to employ you at seventy? They're not going to employ you at sixty-five. I found it hard enough getting a job when I was forty-eight. I'd hate to try and do that today.

John's vulnerability is summed up by one of his colleagues – a 59-year-old man who works in a more senior IT position:

> You've got to be someone who is seen as useful to the company and flexible and able to do lots of stuff. Older people have a lot of experience, and if they can make their colleagues and senior managers understand this in relation to the job in hand, they can be seen as valuable and kept on. But it's very tempting to take the attitude that I've always been a 'whatever', and that's what I do. If the job of 'whatever' ceases, you're out of luck. [See Box 4.2]

Box 4.2: Terry – 'retired', but kept on the payroll

Sometimes older IT employees are valued so highly that they are granted an 'afterlife' when they retire, as consultants selling their expertise back to the company. But as Terry's story illustrates, such relationships do not always work out. Terry used to be a senior electronic engineer at Cable & Wireless, designing the fibre on the company's British telecoms network and vetting suppliers to ensure that they met the right technical standard. He wanted to stay, but was forced to quit in 2000 when he reached C&W's former mandatory retirement age of sixty. 'They didn't want to lose my services, so they said, "The only way you can do this is in fact to form your own company so we can keep you on." So I carried on with my own company for a couple of years after that. I was selling my head to them.'

Terry tried hard to make a success of the new arrangement, working from his home in Reading. But he disliked the pressure of running his own business, as well as the constant travel around Europe to visit C&W's suppliers. 'I came to a point where I put my foot on the ball and said, "What am I doing?" I was now potentially independent, and I thought, "Why am I running around?"' Terry wound up his one-man, one-client consultancy and eventually downsized to a part-time data-processing job at ING Direct bank in Reading. In retrospect, C&W would have done better to keep Terry on staff rather than exposing him to unnecessary stress.

It is, of course, much harder for an older IT worker to avoid being classified as a has-been if his or her manager retains the ageist mindset of the 1990s. It is especially difficult for older IT workers who are employed on contract, with almost no job security, by recruitment agencies. But it is possible to overcome such stereotyping, with sufficient persistence and flexibility.

Joe Woodrow, a 65-year-old former army officer, is one such battle-hardened IT veteran. Bluff and avuncular, Joe enjoys a rural lifestyle, training greyhounds with his wife in the village of Mortimer, ten miles south of Reading. Their cottage is far removed from the European head office of Foster Wheeler, the US engineering multinational, in Reading, where Joe works on contract as a database analyst.

Joe realises that he is not most people's idea of a typical techie. But as he explains, his decision to make a career in technology after he left the army in 1973 represented a natural progression. 'I was in the army for twelve years, and I did [my last] six years on the trot working with computers. I knew that my next tour was going to be a regimental tour. So I figured that it would be sensible for me to move back into civilian life and get a job in computers, because the technology was advancing so quickly by then that after three years I'd be out of date.'

Between 1973 and 1997, Joe worked for various technology companies in the Reading area, eventually becoming a logistics networks consultant at Digital Equipment, the US computer firm. But he was made redundant in 1997, when Digital was taken over by its US rival Compaq (which has itself since been acquired by Hewlett-Packard). Joe was unemployed for the next three years, at the height of the late 1990s technology boom. He says his age was a crucial handicap:

My experience when I finished at Digital was that I probably wrote about 250 letters. I registered with all the agencies, and God knows what, and I got about twelve replies and about one interview. Most of them said, 'You're overqualified.' It was a euphemism for saying, basically, 'I'm a 35-year-old manager, and I don't want a 55-year-old guy working for me.' . . . Eventually I started up my own little business training people on computers on Microsoft Office. It made a few pennies, but not a lot, so in the end I said, 'To hell with this,' and I went down to an employment agency [in Reading] and said I'd like a job.

Fortunately for Joe, the agency was looking to fill a contract position at Foster Wheeler as a computer data analyst for an engineering project. Joe has worked continuously at Foster Wheeler ever since on a series of short-term contracts, apart from a six-month break in 2004–5 for a cataract operation. But he knows that he is always just one project away from possible unemployment. His latest brush with redundancy came in the spring of 2006, when he did not get a new contract until a few weeks before the next job was due to begin.

Given Joe's seemingly comfortable lifestyle, why does he bother with all this professional anxiety?

> For the money. It's as simple and straightforward as that . . . I have got a pension, but it's not a very big one. I had a little trouble with the taxman a few years back and I had to cash in my pension to pay him off. I've still got a small mortgage.

Joe has never persuaded an employer or contractor that his age and consequent expertise are exactly the reasons for hiring him. But this barrier is not insurmountable. Indeed, if IT centres such as Reading really are leading the way towards the Lisbon summit's vaunted 'knowledge economy', the right kind of IT wisdom and experience ought to be sellable in the near future at a premium.

Martin, a 54-year-old former computer programmer, illustrates the point. Since 2003, he has run a one-man web design and marketing consultancy from his Reading home, where he lives with his wife, who works as a teacher, and his teenage son (his daughter is at college). As Martin explains, the business is successful because it capitalises on more than thirty years' experience in the IT industry.

In 1973, Martin graduated from the University of Edinburgh with a degree in mathematics and computer science. He worked for the next ten years as a programmer for various technology companies, until he too was hired in 1983 by Digital Equipment. Martin stayed with Digital for fifteen years, initially as a programmer and then in marketing, working from the group's Reading office. But in 1998 his steady upward career path suddenly veered downhill with the Compaq takeover. Compaq sold Martin's department to a small telecommunications firm in Newbury called Cabletron, which immediately sold the unit again to a telecom start-up called Riverstone. Meanwhile, the global technology industry was going through the worst slump in its history. At the end of 2002 Martin lost his job.

> I was fifty-one at the time. I thought, 'Do I want to put a lot of effort into trying to get a similar job to the one I'd been doing in a collapsing market, where there was probably a 50 per cent chance of getting a job, and then an 80 per cent chance of being in the same position in six months' time, because everybody was getting into trouble?' So I decided that I'd like to do something different and work for myself and have a bit more control over what I was doing.

Martin launched his web design consultancy with two markets in mind. Firstly, he saw an opportunity to design websites for business clients, using his programming skills. Secondly, he thought he could write technical and sales brochures for telecom and computer networking companies, drawing on his marketing background.

> The first six months I earned nothing and put a lot of effort into trying to get work, which is quite difficult when you've no track record. It's a Catch-22 situation. But in the end I found that my biggest and best resource of potential work was all my own contacts. I'd spent the first six months trying to make new contacts, and suddenly realised that the best route was to use my old contacts. Once I started to recultivate them, the business picked up.

The consultancy is now profitable, providing Martin with a comfortable income, with the technical writing side accounting for about 60 per cent of the turnover and the web design for the rest. As a one-man band, working from home, Martin's operating costs are minimal, with the entire business run from his laptop. He says his biggest challenge is maintaining a steady flow of contracts:

> I go through periods when I've a lot on. Then I get slightly complacent and the work stops and I have to go dashing around. I'm not great at planning ahead, because I'm on my own and I can't keep going out and getting new business while doing business at the same time. There are peaks and troughs.

So what is his main selling point? Martin says it is his all-round IT experience, and in particular, his ability to write computer code. As he explains, this skill was commonplace when he began his career in the late 1970s:

> At that time all the banks and insurance companies had great armies of programmers writing programs. And that lasted for about fifteen or twenty years. No-one has hordes of programmers anymore. Everybody just buys what Mr Gates wants to give them, so no-one really does a lot of customisation . . . [But] if you want a very sophisticated website, you have to write a program. So I think that's one advantage I've got. And the other advantage is my marketing experience. I've got the ability to get a message over which gels with what the customer is looking for.

Martin already belongs to the borderless, IT-based economy that Europe's leaders want all their citizens to join. He is also a pension reformer's dream ticket. He has no plans to stop working, even though he and his wife have a reasonable retirement nest egg. They plan to move eventually to somewhere on the south coast, where Martin expects to continue working:

> My intention is definitely to carry on the business. All I need is a broadband link and somewhere to work and I can carry on working anywhere, especially in this market, because the web is going to be even more pervasive. There's always going to be a need for web plumbers.

*

The contrasting experiences of John, Joe Woodrow and Martin suggest that in two crucial respects the IT sector presents the same challenges for an older person as any other labour market. The only difference is that those challenges may be more extreme.

Firstly, it is not true that because the IT industry is plagued with ageism, the sector is therefore hostile to anyone born in the adding-machine era. The reality is more nuanced. Jobseekers and job providers in the IT labour market mutually reinforce ageist stereotypes, just as they do in other sectors from retail to manufacturing. In this context, the case of one HR manager at an IT services company in Reading is telling. She asserts that most employees are burnt out by their fifties, but also complains about a lack of older applicants for vacancies: 'You don't tend to find so many 45-plus people . . . It's not that I would interview someone and say, "I'm not going to offer them a job because of their age." It's just that they're not applying for those kinds of position.'

Secondly, it is not just older IT workers who face the challenge of constantly upgrading and updating their skills if they want to extend their working lives. The challenge is shared by older people in every labour market, regardless of the industry. The technology revolution that has turned Askar Shebani from a garden shed Mr Fixit into a digital millionaire is also transforming business processes across all employment sectors. But as the next chapter shows, this revolution has left a generation of older unskilled workers in its wake. Many, if not most, of them cannot adapt to a world where they must carry a laptop as well as a toolbox.

5   Blue-collar blues

John Daly props his broom in the corner of the construction site canteen, wipes his hands on his overalls and muses on why he is still doing manual work at the age of seventy-eight.

> The doctor says he preferred that I keep working and not to stay at home. He says I'd seize up. I often think I'm going to be working till I drop down, you know. All my friends who started work when I did are all bloody dead, would you believe it.

A stocky man with thick, black-framed spectacles, John has been an unskilled labourer in Reading's building industry since he emigrated from Ireland in 1967. His latest job involves sweeping up after the other workers on a residential development next to Tesco's main Reading supermarket. John earns just over £250 for a six-day week. While the money is a welcome supplement to his small state pension, he reckons he and his wife will have enough to get by when he finally retires. 'The job keeps my wheels turning, but I expect that in the next six to twelve months, I will definitely pack it in. The trouble is that if I were sitting at home I'd get bored.'

With no trade qualifications, John is a relic from an industrial past that is fast disappearing from the manufacturing centres of Europe.

Until the 1970s, towns such as Reading were full of jobs for manual workers who had little to sell but their muscles. In Reading they shifted goods round warehouses, dug holes in the ground for the gas board or, like John, heaved bricks for builders. Today, such jobs are generally automated and require a range of technical skills that frequently include basic computer literacy. And those lower-grade manual jobs that remain are increasingly being taken by migrant labourers from the new EU member states in eastern Europe who are willing to work for low pay. When John finally hands in his broom, he is likely to be replaced by a Pole with a brush.

In one sense, John is fortunate. His career is ending just as he is losing his residual selling power in a rapidly changing labour market. The unlucky ones are the millions of older blue-collar men* who have fallen out of employment for various reasons, but still desperately need an income to achieve a secure retirement.

In Britain, as throughout the developed world, unemployment afflicts poorer, older people disproportionately. According to the Department for Education and Skills, 40 per cent of 'workless' people in 2003 in the fifty-plus age group were in the lowest wealth quintile for all age groups, while 57 per cent were in households with no occupational pension.† The plight of poorer, older men was highlighted by a survey in 2002–3 of more than 12,000 respondents for the English Longitudinal Study of Ageing (ELSA) which reported a gulf between the employment rates of older men in different income groups. In the lowest wealth quintile, more than 40 per cent of men between fifty and fifty-four said they were 'economically inactive'; the proportion rose to about 50 per cent for the 55–59 age group, and more than 60 per cent for the 60–64 age

---

*The next chapter considers the situation of older women in the labour market.
†*Challenging Age: Information, Advice and Guidance for Older Age Groups* (Department for Education and Skills, 2003), p. 5.

group. By comparison, about 20 per cent of all men in the other four wealth quintiles were economically inactive in their fifties, rising to about 45 per cent in their early sixties.*

The tendency of older unskilled men to lose touch with the world of work is compounded by three factors. Firstly, many of them subscribe to an entrenched culture of early retirement. A separate ELSA survey found that men in their fifties in the bottom wealth decile reported on average only a 37.3 per cent chance of still working at sixty, compared with an overall average for all income groups of 55.3 per cent.[†] While some expect to lose their jobs, others will almost certainly quit because they do not like working. Philip Taylor, Professor of Ageing and Social Policy at Swinburne University, Australia, says this is a reasonable attitude to take if you have spent a career doing dreary, repetitive manual labour: '[With] whole swathes of the working population who are in low-paid, low-skilled jobs, can you really conceive of a scenario where many of these people will be working on for longer? It may be good for them, but will they want to, and can they?'

Secondly, this early retirement culture has been reinforced by the unchecked growth in the number of older men (and women) who quit work for health reasons, start claiming incapacity benefit and never return to employment. In 2005, the Department for Work and Pensions (DWP) estimated that there were about 1.3 million people on incapacity benefit in the 50–64 age group, of whom almost half had been claiming for at least five

*Michael Marmot, James Banks, Richard Blundell, Carli Lessof and James Nazroo (eds), *Health, Wealth and Lifestyles of the Older Population in England: The 2002 English Longitudinal Study of Ageing* (London: Institute for Fiscal Studies, 2004), Fig. 4.3.

[†]James Banks, Carl Emmerson, Zoë Oldfield and Gemma Tetlow, *Prepared for Retirement?: The Adequacy and Distribution of Retirement Resources in England* (London: Institute for Fiscal Studies, 2005), p. ii.

years.* A disproportionate number had left blue-collar jobs. According to research by the DWP, in 2004

> far higher proportions of older people [between fifty and the state pension age] who worked as process, plant and machine operatives (30 per cent) and in skilled trade occupations (29 per cent) were inactive for health reasons than those who worked in managerial or senior occupations, and professional occupations (both 15 per cent).†

This is the backdrop to the government's plans to reform the incapacity benefit system by gearing it towards getting claimants back into work.

Thirdly, older people (especially men) with poor qualifications are least likely to 'train up' to get the necessary skills that will make them more employable. In the winter of 2005/6, the UK Labour Force Survey reported that only 16.6 per cent of employees between fifty and the state pension age were receiving job-related training, compared with 23.7 per cent of the 25–34 age group, and 38.6 per cent of workers between thirty-five and forty-nine.‡

All these problems are found at Thames Water, the former state-owned utility with head offices in Reading. Richard Newcombe, Thames Water's head of training and development, curses the early retirement packages that were introduced by the company after privatisation in 1985 in order to slim down its bloated workforce. In

* House of Commons Committee of Public Accounts, *Welfare to Work: Tackling the Barriers to the Employment of Older People*, tenth report, Session 2004–05, HC 439, p. 6.

† Roger Morgan, 'Older People and the Labour Market', in A. Soule, Penny Babb, Maria Evandrou, Stephen Balchin and Linda Zealey (eds), *Focus on Older People*, 2005 edn (London: National Statistics, 2005), p. 35.

‡ *Labour Force Survey Historical Quarterly Supplement* (London: National Statistics), Table 28a.

2006, it was still possible for a long-standing employee at Thames Water to retire in his early fifties with a generous severance deal. As a result, less than 10 per cent of the company's 5,371 employees had more than ten years' service with the company and were also over the age of fifty-five.*

Newcombe says it is a waste of resources to pour all this experience down the drain. Despite plans by Thames Water to cut a quarter of its staff by 2010, he would like to build up a talent pool of seasoned company veterans.

There are many employees who have been with the company for twenty or thirty years or more. Some believe that they are going to be able to retire in their early fifties. We may well need to say to them that we don't want you to retire early. We need your knowledge and skills.'

However, Newcombe adds that there is another group of older employees who will need to upgrade their skills simply to keep their jobs, which require far more technical expertise than when they started their careers. And here, he says, he is hitting an unmovable psychological barrier.

Nowadays, a person who works in a treatment works has got to be more computer literate and good with systems operations and other forms of new technology. I suspect there are still people hanging on [with insufficient skills], but ultimately they are going to struggle. We've had literacy and numeracy programmes, but it has been very difficult to get people to come forward and say, 'Please help me,' even though we will pay for it all.

*Company information.

The view of Newcombe and other HR managers about the low training participation rates of older workers is not shared by the trade unions. Nor is it shared by Patrick Grattan, chief executive of The Age and Employment Network:

> There is widespread recognition of the payback from training, and from employing older people. Yet the vast majority of businesses are not offering older people training. There's a fear that if you train people they will leave you and move on. Actually, the evidence shows that retention rates in businesses that invest in career development and training are stronger.

Regardless of who is to blame, nobody disputes the outcome: a rump of underskilled older blue-collar workers of doubtful economic value to any employer.

Sue Culver, counsellor at the TEA Shop in Reading, tries to help these people at her weekly job club for the over-fifties, which is mostly attended by older, unemployed men from blue-collar backgrounds. To an outsider, the advice dispensed by Culver seems very basic. She stresses the importance of looking in the classified section of Reading's two main newspapers for job advertisements, as well as checking the window displays in the town's many recruitment agencies. Then she asks whether anyone goes on the internet to look for vacancies and is met by a sullen silence.

Afterwards, Culver explains that the hardest task is getting inside her clients' heads. 'I try to change their attitude and the way they are looking for work, because it isn't the same as what it was years ago. You could see a postcard, go in the window, someone would apply, and there'd be no other applicants.' Culver tries in particular to persuade her clients that they need to improve their skills:

I think older people are keen to be trained, but it's a question of how you do it. For a lot of people, their memories are of school, where they were told, 'You can't do that, you're useless, go to the back of the class.' Some people come with so much baggage that you've got all of that to contend with. So you tell them that education these days isn't like it used to be, and you try to encourage them to want to learn.

The stumbling block for many of her clients is an almost primal fear of computers. At this job club session, one unemployed factory worker asserts defensively that he has managed perfectly alright for fifty-seven years without using a computer, and does not intend to change the habit of a lifetime. As Culver observes later, that attitude instantly disqualifies him from most low-grade industrial work in Reading. 'These days, even warehousemen are asked, "Can you enter these figures onto a computer?" and you've got to be able to say yes. But some older people say, "I'm not sure," because they're scared and they haven't done it before.'

One job club member in particular epitomises the challenge faced not only by Culver, but by politicians and academics addressing the problem of long-term unemployment among older blue-collar men. Patrick, a burly 58-year-old Irish expatriate, has not had permanent work since 1998, when he resigned as a shift foreman at a company near Reading that made extrusion plastics, after the firm relocated to the north-east of England. Most days Patrick – who is divorced with four grown-up children – sits in his dingy, one-bedroomed flat in Reading, watching television beneath a picture of Pope John Paul II that sits on his well-stocked drinks cabinet. This lifestyle is financed by Patrick's jobseeker's allowance of 'just under £100 per week', of which about half goes to pay his mortgage.

Patrick's story is a salutary tale about being overtaken by a fast-changing economy. He spent twenty-five years with the plastics company, and at his income peak in the mid-1990s was earning £31,000 a year for a punishing 84-hour week that included regular night shifts (a factor, he says, in the collapse of his marriage). When his firm moved to Darlington at the end of 1998 – partly to benefit from the north-east's cheaper labour market – Patrick was told that as a long-standing employee he could keep his job if he were willing to move as well.

I went to Darlington about six months later and could see straightaway that the business was in trouble. What was the point in me stopping up there, knowing I was going to get made redundant again? I'd put this place [his present flat in east Reading] on the market, and I was going to move up there permanently. I near enough ended losing this place as well. I worked up there for nearly four months, but I could see what was happening.

Patrick returned to Reading, armed with a letter of reference from the company's managing director. Proudly, he produces it from a drawer.

It says, 'He has performed his tasks with enthusiasm and diligence, often working without direct supervision . . . [and] possesses a high degree of skill and is able to work with many different types of extrusion machine. He has good management skills and is able to pass on his experience to younger members of staff.'

Patrick set about looking for a job that matched what he felt were his qualifications and consequent salary level. He failed completely. Since coming back to Reading in 1999, Patrick has been employed for a total of seven discontinuous months in two temporary jobs:

cleaning machinery in the press room of a local newspaper, and sorting letters for a mail order firm. The latter company wanted him to stay, but Patrick did not like the money. 'What I'm after is a job that is going to pay me £8 an hour. I'd be quite happy on £8 an hour. I know I could pay my mortgage and council tax and things like that.'

The most troubling aspect of Patrick's story is that in the old industrial economy, he genuinely did possess 'a high degree of skill'. As he points out, he was not only a skilled mechanic, but supervised about a dozen other workers. Patrick thus stands above less qualified frequenters of the various fifty-plus job clubs at the Reading TEA Shop such as Roy (see Chapter 1) and Clive (see Chapter 2).

Yet Patrick's industrial credentials count for little in the modern labour market. The easy explanation, which Patrick trots out in his bleaker moments, is that he is the victim of ageism. The reality is that any ageist prejudice encountered by Patrick is amplified by his own inability to make two crucial adjustments to the new world of work. His insistence on holding out for a job that pays £8 an hour demonstrates an unrealistic idea of his earning power. This attitude is common among many older unemployed blue-collar workers, who treat their last wage packet as a benchmark for future employers.

Patrick is also averse to learning elementary computer skills, such as sending an e-mail, that would give him a better chance of earning £8 an hour. So far, he has resisted the suggestion that he should enrol on one of the TEA Shop's computer training courses.

They've actually asked me that and, yeah, I might take them on, provided they're willing to pay for it. I'm still thinking about it. You know, going into computers is something that you've got to work at from an early age and that. So when you're my age, I think it does frighten you that little bit.

Patrick stubs out his cigarette angrily, unable to disguise his frustration.

I come from a big family north of Dublin and I started work at fourteen and I never stopped working till I was made redundant. I hear a lot of people complaining now about doing a 35-hour week. But I used to work an 84-hour week, so whatever my working span, I've actually worked forty-four years, because I was doing two weeks' work for their one week.

*

How can men like Patrick find a footing in the modern labour market? The government has attacked the problem of long-term unemployment among older, poorly qualified men from numerous angles, in common with other EU countries. In 2000 it launched New Deal 50 Plus, a programme aimed at people over fifty who have been out of work for at least six months and are claiming benefits. In 2005 the then Work and Pensions Secretary, Alan Johnson, introduced plans to reform incapacity benefit, with the bulk of less sick claimants facing a reduction in their allowance if they did not attend interviews designed to get them back into employment. (The proposals form part of the government's welfare to work Bill which will be debated by Parliament in 2007.)

Experts from front-line job counsellors such as Sue Culver to Whitehall policymakers agree that education in its broadest sense – including retraining and the teaching of basic job-hunting skills – is the key to improving the employment prospects of older blue-collar workers. In this context, campaigners for older workers' rights were hopeful that the Leitch Review of Skills, which delivered its final report in December 2006, would signal a new government approach to lifelong learning in the workplace.* Their hopes have not been fulfilled.

The review – commissioned by Gordon Brown and conducted by Lord Leitch, the former chief executive of Zurich Financial Services – acknowledges the need to reduce the skills deficit among older people, given that demographic trends will limit the number of younger people entering the workforce between now and 2020. Thus his interim report, published in December 2005, drew attention to the fact that 25 per cent of all people in the 55–64 age group have no qualifications, compared with only 10 per cent of 25–34-year-olds.[†]

As the interim report observed, 'the skills of young people alone will not improve the UK's overall skills profile significantly enough by 2020'. This is because 70 per cent of 2020's working-age population have already completed their compulsory school education, and half of 2020's working-age population is already over twenty-five years old – beyond the age when people are likely to take the conventional education route from school through to higher education. Leitch further noted that by 2020, adults aged 50–65 years will account for 60 per cent of the growth in the working age population. 'The contribution of older people to the labour market will become increasingly important. By 2020, 30 per cent of the working age population will be over 50, compared with 25 per cent today. These demographic changes make it essential to improve the skills of older groups in the workforce.'[‡]

Unfortunately, the final report – while repeating this analysis – is

---

* *Prosperity for All in the Global Economy – World Class Skills: Final Report* (Leitch Review of Skills) (Treasury, 2006).
[†] *Skills in the UK: The Long-Term Challenge: Interim Report* (Norwich: HMSO, 2005), p. 8.
[‡] Ibid.

short of detailed prescriptions about how to tackle the problem. The Leitch review thus looks destined to join numerous other initiatives, reports and studies in recent years by both government and employers that have failed to improve Britain's dismal record on the training of older people. It is hardly good news that Britain's record in this regard is actually better than most developed countries, according to data published by the OECD in 2006.* This mediocre achievement merely highlights how older, low-skilled workers across the OECD area are falling through the training and education net.

Part of the solution is to spend more on training resources for the fifty-plus age group. Alan Pickering, an expert on pensions and the older workforce at Watson Wyatt, the human resources consultancy, accuses successive governments of short-changing older people on this front, just as businesses have skimped on training: 'We need to reallocate our training spending across the age spectrum . . . and spend it more evenly through people's working lives. Eighteen-year-olds are going to need retraining when they're twenty-eight, thirty-eight, forty-eight or fifty-eight.' Such a shift in training resources will prove difficult to sell, despite the plethora of programmes to help older people. At a recent seminar on sustaining working lives beyond fifty, one senior civil servant remarked that the government's skills strategy was focused on younger people – and that the experts on the older workforce around the table had better get used to that fact.

More money for training older people is not the whole solution, however. In particular, as Pickering points out, improving the delivery of training programmes for people over fifty will not help older, unemployed blue-collar workers who have become so demoralised that they have effectively dropped out of the labour market. It is telling that in 2005, 38 per cent of all people in Britain on incapacity

*_Live Longer, Work Longer_ (Paris: OECD, 2006), p. 75.

benefit were eligible because of mental health problems. Many of them were on a familiar downward slide from intolerable workplace stress to the depression of long-term unemployment. This condition is of course not limited to people on incapacity benefit. The listlessness common to older, unemployed blue-collar workers such as Patrick and Clive (see Chapter 2), neither of whom has claimed incapacity benefit, reveals deep, unliftable gloom. They are almost, if not completely, impossible to rescue from their predicament.

*

There is, however, a more hopeful side to this story, which illustrates how different worlds of work are converging in the modern labour market. Across Europe, there is high demand for suitably qualified blue-collar workers in a range of sectors, from plumbing to construction (see Box 5.1). Thus Reading, like the rest of Britain, has been inundated in recent years with young migrant workers from eastern Europe. They have mopped up much of the unskilled and semi-skilled trade and building work in the town by undercutting local workmen on price. In the process, they have been blamed for stealing local jobs.

Look more closely at Reading's blue-collar labour market and a more complex picture emerges. Local employers still chase skilled older craftsmen such as the four builders at Purley Magna (see Chapter 1) and indeed anyone who has the right combination of age, experience and maturity. This point is underlined in Reading not only by HR managers like Richard Newcombe at Thames Water, but by recruitment agencies that specialise in industrial vacancies. Jake Esman, who runs the Reading branch of Randstad, a Dutch recruitment multinational, says he has no difficulty placing older men with the right qualifications:

Let's take van drivers. There's a lot of van damage with young drivers, who are fairly reckless and unpredictable. If you take an experienced van driver who's not overexcited about racing a van through town but just gets the job done, he gets paid the same but he is more stable and therefore has a higher chance of getting his number of drops done. And also, of course, the people who are making those hiring decisions in the industrial sector are the ones who've often come through the ranks from a van driver to a supervisor to a depot manager. They're in their mid-fifties themselves, and have no real objection to hiring somebody in the same age category.

Box 5.1: Brian Appleby – joining the trade at seventy-five

At the age of sixty-seven, Brian Appleby was tired of his job as a sales director in Ireland for Kleenezee, a Bristol household products firm. He came back to Reading, near where he was born, and with money in the bank developed a serious golf habit. But his retirement was put on hold in 2005, at the age of seventy-three, when his eldest son died.

A widower, Brian has a second son, Ian, who has been profoundly deaf since birth. 'In 2005, he had been unemployed for about six years, and I took an interest in him in a way that I never did before. I think maybe because of my concern with my first son, it made me think along the lines of my second son. What had I done for him? I could see he was going nowhere, because of his disability.'

Brian sat down with Ian shortly after his eldest son's funeral and asked him how he could help. 'He said, "Well, you can help me get a job, but nobody seems to take any interest in me because of my disability." So immediately I said, "Well, how would you like to work for yourself?" But the point is that there is no way he can communicate with people. He hasn't got the push maybe to negotiate a contract or get a business job. So I said,

> "Okay, if I do your paperwork, and you do the hard work, we can start a business."'
>
> Seizing on the fact that Ian was a trained carpenter, Brian decided to start a kitchen-fitting service in the Reading area that competed on price with local migrant workers from eastern Europe. The business was launched in the spring of 2006, and within a few weeks, Brian won an order from Möben, an international kitchen firm, to act as a subcontractor in the Reading area. Ian and his friend Euan are installing one kitchen a week, but Brian says there is far more demand than he can satisfy. 'If I could get the manpower, I could do ten kitchens a week. It's my big, big bugbear.'

It could be argued that van driving is not very skilful. But most of the numerous vacancies for such positions in Reading assume a basic ability to log deliveries and update schedules on a laptop or a personal digital assistant (PDA). Some drivers are also expected to communicate by e-mail with a central database while they are out on the road. These criteria instantly rule out older unskilled men such as Patrick (who in any case cannot drive) and Clive.

The further one climbs up the skills ladder, the more older men from traditional manual occupations benefit from the same information and technology revolution that has pushed their less qualified contemporaries to the margins of the labour market. Stephen McNair observes: 'The amount of work that requires hard physical labour has declined enormously. The other thing that helps in lots of jobs is the accumulation of know-how. You learn ways of doing things, and you simply get better at spotting short cuts.'

Reading's construction industry is a prime example of this trend, exemplified by the four builders at Purley Magna. Paul Wells, the Reading branch manager of Daniel Owen, a specialist agency supplying the local building trade, says there is growing demand for seasoned personnel in senior hard-hat jobs:

> I think probably companies have become softer on the question of employing the older generation over the last eight years or so. When I first came into the industry the emphasis was very much on finding young whippersnappers with lots of energy and drive and saying we don't want any of the old duffers. Now, obviously, there is a massive skills shortage and companies are more understanding. They do realise that they need to look at the people at the other end of the age scale who are able to run the business.

Wells says one reason why older builders are highly prized is because of a steady outflow of foremen, site managers and construction engineers in their fifties who want to retire early. 'Construction is obviously quite a hard industry, so pretty much by fifty-five most people have had enough and really are looking to try and wind down. But that's very much an individual issue. You get old sixty-year-olds, and you get very young sixty-year-olds.'

Mervyn Carter, one of Wells's building site managers, is a very young 68-year-old. After a long day at a luxury residential development near Newbury, he explains why he is possibly the only great-grandfather working in Britain's construction industry:

> There's nothing I like to do better than to go to work, particularly on a new job, or a refurb, and get the drawings out, and have a look at them and say, 'Well, that won't work, that's not right, that's not right, we can't do that there,' and that sort of thing. I just love it. I'll probably shrivel up and die when I stop.

A big, barrel-chested man, Mervyn's original ambition was to be a professional footballer. He had a trial with Portsmouth, but he was not quite good enough and instead became an apprentice with a local building firm. This training has served him well. 'I wouldn't expect anyone to do anything that I wouldn't do myself. In my position, I can do most of the work that the trades do, apart from electrical work. I can do plumbing, I can do carpentry, I can lay bricks.'

Mervyn is clear that it is his all-round know-how that keeps him in such high demand.

There's no substitute for experience. I remember working for one company which I joined through an agency. When I went for the interview, I said, 'I didn't see any advertisement.' He said, 'No, I don't advertise, because you'll get any Tom, Dick and Harry replying to an advert. He may be some kiddie who's sixteen or seventeen, who think they know everything.' He said, 'I want somebody experienced like yourself.'

The husband of a nurse, Mervyn has never let ill health keep him away from the building site for too long. He had three heart attacks in 1988, 'one after the other', but was back at work within a few weeks.

I did have a shock a year ago last May. I had a skin cancer on the left thigh. So I went and had it off in Basingstoke hospital, and the doctor said she wanted me to see a skin specialist in Salisbury, and he said, 'Right, we're going to do a big one and take a lot more off.' That didn't deter me. I said to my wife when I was at home after the operation, 'I can't stand this, I want to go back to work.' And I got up to work one morning, got up too quick, and there was blood pouring down my leg. So I had to have nursing and then, lo and behold, what do I get? MRSA. I picked it up in the hospital in Salisbury where I had the operation. That meant six weeks of very, very strong antibiotics, but then it hung about and hung about. I was having to take a dressing with me to work and do the dressing. But I still didn't want to stop work.

Despite a 'disappointing' personal pension, Mervyn says he does not need to work for the money. He was recently asked by the construction director on his latest project how long he wanted to carry on. 'I said, "Well, if I feel as well when I'm seventy as I do now, I shall continue until I feel it's time that I've had enough."'

*

The most interesting aspect of Mervyn Carter's story is not his ability to bounce back from illnesses that would have finished the career of most people his age. It is the fact that ultimately, the processes he uses to perform his job place him firmly in the new 'knowledge economy'. It is true that he prefers a strong cup of tea rather than a latte in the morning, and that when he gets back to his home in north Hampshire in the evening, he goes to the pub rather than a wine bar. But during his working day, Mervyn explains that he spends most of his time on a computer looking at spreadsheets and using software to refine the building works schedule.

This is the new workplace that is effectively barred to millions of older men from industrial backgrounds whose skills belong to the past. The challenge met by their abler peers is no different from the challenge faced by older men in sectors from retailing to engineering that are being transformed by information technology: to adapt to a labour market where the traditional separation of white-collar brain from blue-collar brawn is rapidly breaking down.

6   The work–life
        imbalance

Older women face the same challenge in the modern labour market as older men. But they have the additional burden of past prejudices and assumptions about their social and economic role.

Jan Duffy is typical of many older women who carry this legacy through their working lives. Five mornings a week, Jan gets on her bike and cycles two miles from her home in the eastern suburb of Woodley to the University of Reading's Bulmershe campus, where she has a part-time job cleaning the student hostels. The job pays about £400 a month. Jan is sixty-nine and suffers from arthritis, and while she says the physical labour helps oil her joints, that is not her main reason for working. 'I'm not doing this job for the love of it, that's for sure. If I wasn't working, I'd have to start going through my savings.'

Jan belongs to an army of older women with low incomes who do menial part-time jobs to bring in a bit more money. In a recent survey of twenty-one OECD member states, proportionately more women did part-time work in Britain than in any other country apart from the Netherlands (see Figure 6.1). And as Jan's story illustrates, they are doubly disadvantaged in the workplace both by their social and economic status, and by their gender.

Born in Glasgow, Jan left school at fifteen with no formal qualifications. Seven years later she moved to Berkshire, when her

Figure 6.1: Part-time work by age and gender as a percentage of all workers by age and gender (2004 data)

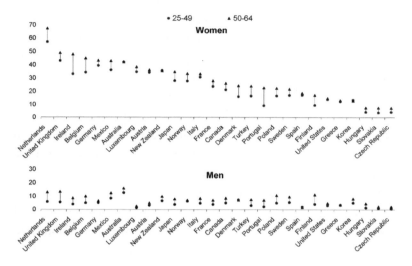

Part-time workers are defined as workers who usually work fewer than 30 hours a week. For Japan and Korea, the data refer to actual hours of work. Source: Fig. 3.13 in *Ageing and Employment Policies: Live Longer, Work Longer*, p. 80 © OECD 2006.

husband got a job near Reading. She has spent the whole of her adult life doing low-grade manual work, except between 1961 and 1969, when she was looking after her four young children. Jan's later career has been overshadowed by increasing job insecurity, in common with many unskilled industrial workers of both sexes. From 1969 to 1998 she worked on the production line at Huntley, Boorne & Stevens, the now-defunct Reading biscuit tin manufacturer. But in 1998, at the age of sixty-two, Jan was made redundant when the factory moved to Wales, where labour was cheaper.

Her immediate financial situation was barely affected by losing her job so close to retirement, because she received statutory redundancy pay. Jan had a bigger long-term headache. She is one of about 100,000 older married women who chose to pay the so-called 'small stamp', reduced national insurance contribution for wives, until it was abolished in 1977. Successive post-war governments blithely assumed that women such as Jan on the 'small stamp' would be able to rely chiefly on their husband's retirement income in old age. Jan – whose husband retired early from the building trade for health reasons – regrets her mistake. 'It was my own fault. I had the option to take the full stamp or a married woman's stamp, and at the time I didn't realise that it would affect the state pension. Otherwise I would have paid the full stamp.'

Under the present benefits regime, Jan can top up her reduced basic state pension (BSP) of about £50 per week by claiming a means-tested pension credit that will increase her total BSP allowance. She also has a very small personal pension scheme, worth about £35 per month, which she began after she left Huntley, Boorne & Stevens. But given her past low earnings and lack of savings, she says she still needs to work (and thus forgo the pension credit) to enjoy reasonable financial security in old age. 'If I stopped work now, we'd have much, much less to live on.'

Pedalling into work every morning, Jan is one figure in a discouraging labour market for women over fifty. In July 2006, 68.8 per cent of women between fifty and their state pension age of sixty were in full-time or part-time employment, compared with 72.4 per cent of men between fifty and sixty-five.* That is not a huge gender gap. Even so, more than thirty years after the 1975 Sex

---

* *First Release: Labour Market Statistics, September 2006* (London: National Statistics, 2006), Table 2. The statistics do not report the employment rate for men between fifty and sixty.

Discrimination Act, older British women – like their counterparts in other OECD countries – generally have fewer job opportunities and are paid less than their male counterparts.

In 2003/4, the Department for Work and Pensions reported that women aged 55–59 had an average median income of just under £150 per week, 42 per cent of the average income of men in the same age group.* The majority of women also leave the labour market at a younger age than men. In a 2002–3 survey for the English Longitudinal Study of Ageing, 61 per cent of women in the 55–59 age group said they were 'economically active', as did 30 per cent of women in the 60–64 age group. The comparable figures for men were 73 per cent and 48 per cent respectively (with the latter figure certainly increased by the higher male state pension age).†

It is certain that the employment gap between older men and women will be narrowed as the state pension age for women gradually rises from sixty to sixty-five between 2010 and 2020. Yet women who want to extend their careers will still be at a disadvantage, because the challenges they face in the labour market are not solely connected with work. They are also linked to wider family and caring responsibilities. Above all, they are tied to the continuing influence on older women's professional lives of earlier typecasting as second-class citizens.

Sue Yeandle, Professor of Sociology at the University of Leeds, concludes from extensive research into older women and the workplace that the legacy of the past is one of the biggest hindrances to later career success.

*Family Resources Survey (Department for Work and Pensions, 2005).
†Michael Marmot, James Banks, Richard Blundell, Carli Lessof and James Nazroo (eds), Health, Wealth and Lifestyles of the Older Population in England: The 2002 English Longitudinal Study of Ageing (London: Institute for Fiscal Studies, 2004), Fig. 4.3.

Opportunities in the labour market are highly structured for men. Everybody has always assumed that, irrespective of their family position, men should be in the labour market. On the other hand . . . lots of women who are now in their fifties had to take a break. If they're at the bottom end of their fifties, they'll have just scraped in on maternity rights legislation. But the older generation wouldn't have had maternity leave options. It would have been an odd thing to do and all of your family would have thought you were a bit strange. So most of them would have taken a period out of the labour market, and then, unless they'd had a very high-powered career, they would have taken a back seat to their husbands.

As Yeandle points out, many women over fifty had to overcome a wall of prejudice within their families just to be able to work. Jane Watts, a sixty-year-old staff nurse at the Royal Berkshire Hospital in Reading, testifies to how such pressure altered the course of her career. Born in Reading, Jane always wanted to be a nurse from when she was a child.

It was a lifelong ambition. My sister was a nurse, and I was planning to become a nurse at eighteen. The date was set, 9 February, but I had met what's now my husband . . . I can remember him sitting in the car and saying, 'Well, we might as well finish now, because I shall never see you if you do nursing.' I should have turned round and said, 'Well, stuff you, then,' but I didn't.

Jane abandoned her aim to be a nurse, and spent several years instead working as an assistant in a dental practice. She stopped work to bring up her two sons, and then became a pharmacy technician. At the age of forty-five, Jane completed a National Vocational Qualification course and became a health care assistant for the Royal

Berkshire and Battle Hospital Trust. Two years later, Jane decided that she wanted to realise her original ambition and applied to the trust to train to become a nurse. She still bristles at the memory. 'They said I was too late. They didn't want to know. They pushed me aside, so I said, "Oh, blow you lot then."'

Six years after that, at the age of fifty-three, Jane tried again. This time the trust was much more supportive, partly because of growing concern within the NHS about a national shortage of qualified nurses. 'I thought they wouldn't have me because they'd think I was too old. But in actual fact they seconded me to do it. I didn't have to go on a bursary, and I continued to have my wages, and qualified when I was fifty-seven.'

Jane's husband, who works on the maintenance team at Reading prison, has long since acknowledged he was wrong to stop her becoming a nurse. 'He has been absolutely, categorically wonderful, because I think he's always felt he stopped me, and I think he did. And he knew how I regretted it over the years. So my boys were grown up and had left home, and he just bent over backwards to support me.'

Unlike many nurses who retire early, Jane intends to carry on until she is sixty-five to compensate for her late start.

At fifty I thought my life was over. I was working as a health care assistant and that was it. I was just waiting to die. And then I trained to be a nurse and all this happened to me since then. For months after qualifying, all of a sudden I'd look at my husband and say, 'I'm a nurse!' And he used to say, 'I know you are.' So in that latter part of my life I feel I've achieved more than in the previous fifty years. I can go to my grave happy.

It is not just straightforward prejudice such as Jane encountered which undermines the careers of many older women. In addition, their professional opportunities are often restricted because they failed to realise their educational potential in an era when many parents assumed that their career would be cut short by children. This educational deficit is illustrated by the relative level of qualifications among older women and older men. Only 10 per cent of women in the 55–64 age group have at least one A-level or an equivalent qualification, compared with about a third of their male contemporaries; and over a third of women in this age group have no qualifications, compared with about a quarter of their male peers (see Box 6.1).*

Box 6.1: Joan Whyte – the well-educated secretary

Some older women can thank their parents for having a more enlightened approach to the education of their daughters. Joan Whyte's father ran a greengrocer's shop in Reigate, Surrey after the Second World War. In the normal course of events Joan (now fifty-eight) and her sister might have been expected to leave school at fifteen, like millions of other girls from their modest background. Instead, their parents had higher ambitions for them. 'It's quite surprising. My family were working class, but my parents fortunately saw education for girls as useful. So both my sister and I went to university in the 1960s.'

Joan graduated in history from Royal Holloway College, part of the University of London. Her subsequent career took a more conventional route for married women of her generation. She juggled bringing up her two sons with part-time work as a laboratory assistant and then as a secretary at Reading University. Meanwhile, her husband pursued a full-time career at the government Meteorological Office in nearby Bracknell. Joan still works

---

* Women and Work Commission, *Shaping a Fairer Future* (Department of Trade and Industry, 2006), p. 51.

four days a week as a secretary in the university's Italian department, and has no regrets about putting family before work when her children were young. 'There's no way I'd have taken a full-time job, because I think it's important that mothers are at home.'

Janet Tabatabai, a 55-year-old part-time receptionist at the Reading campus of Thames Valley University (TVU), is one of many older women who were short-changed educationally. Sitting in TVU's noisy cafeteria, she recalls the expectations that were placed on her as a teenager growing up in Exeter, where her father was based as a commercial traveller and her mother worked as a shop assistant. 'In my time, if you weren't married by about twenty-odd, you were on the shelf.'

Janet left school at sixteen with five O-levels and went to Exeter Technical College, where she took a course in office administration and typing. 'I don't think anybody considered that I might go to university. My brother went to university, but in those days the girls did the secretarial course.' Janet then spent two years as a secretary at Barclays Bank in Exeter, but stopped in 1971, following the birth of her first daughter. She and her partner, an Iranian expatriate, married in 1973. Janet continued to do part-time secretarial work until they moved to Reading in 1983, when she decided to devote herself full-time to bringing up their children while her husband built up his computer consultancy business.

In 1990, 'feeling a bit bored', Janet enrolled at the age of thirty-nine on a return-to-work course at Reading College (which eventually became part of TVU in 2004). The experience put her off further education. 'Nothing much came of it, really. I didn't enjoy the IT all that much, to be honest, and I didn't really know how I was going to apply it. I think I'd lost a lot of confidence as well. I didn't feel confident enough to go into the workplace.' Nonetheless, shortly after finishing the course, Janet took a part-time Christmas job at the Reading branch of Toys 'R' Us, working in customer services. The job was extended, and Janet stayed with Toys 'R' Us for the next ten years. Then in 2000, with her two youngest children now teenagers, Janet reviewed her career again. She decided to enrol on a general office administration course at Reading College, which was a much more rewarding experience, leading directly to her present job at TVU (as it has become) as a part-time receptionist.

Surrounded by students less than half her age, Janet has also caught the education bug. In the summer of 2006 she successfully completed an 'access to university' course at TVU. She plans to start a full university degree at TVU in 2008, possibly in philosophy. Meanwhile, Janet aims to save as much as possible from her income to help fund her future studies. 'I've been using money mostly for my children. Now perhaps it's time to do something for myself.' Unlike many mature students, Janet does not think her degree will be the launch pad for a new career. 'By the time I finish the course, I think I'll be too close to the pension age.'

Listening to Janet, it is easy to conclude that she must be bitter about missed career opportunities resulting from an inferior education. Yet her interpretation of her life story is not so simple, in common with many women her age. Janet would doubtless have had the prospect of a more rewarding career if she had followed her brother to university. But she is emphatic that spending most of her twenties and thirties as a full-time wife and mother was the best choice for her, as well as her children.

I loved my time at home, I really loved it. I'm very lucky I could have done it, really. In fact, I think it was the best time of my life. I loved bringing my kids up. I would just never have wanted them to come home with nobody there to make sure they were safe.

Such views, shared by millions of women of Janet's age, are sometimes portrayed as meek acceptance of their inferior status in relation to husbands who go out to work. The implied contrast is with a younger generation of career women, who try to juggle both work and family commitments. But as Janet points out, older women who want to return to work after having a family often undersell themselves to employers. 'You forget about all the skills that you've got as a mother, like communication skills. You forget about your time-keeping skills, and even your personality. You forget about all those skills that you've got to offer, which a lot of the younger generation don't have.'

Indeed, many women never leave caring responsibilities behind them, even after their children have grown up (see Box 6.2). As the children leave home, sick or elderly relatives and then spouses can start to claim more of their time. Here is another way in which the later careers of older women can be restricted and, in many cases, halted.

It is difficult to underestimate the scale of this issue, which also affects men. According to the 2001 census, one in four women in the 50–59 age group provide some form of unpaid care, compared with just under one in five men in the same cohort.* It is the peak age for caring, with the proportion of carers declining to just over one in ten of all adults aged sixty-five or over. Overall, a study in 2004 for the charity Age Concern calculated that unpaid carers saved the British economy about £15 billion per year.†

* *Facts about Carers* (London: Carers UK, 2005), p. 2.
† Pamela Meadows and Volterra Consulting, *The Economic Contribution of Older People* (London: Age Concern, 2004), p. 35.

Box 6.2: Dorothy – working to look after her grandson

Four days a week, Dorothy works as an accounts executive at a Reading department store. After a long career in office management, she is surprised to find herself still doing a demanding job at the age of sixty-seven. 'I didn't visualise that I would still be working at this age, ever. But then it comes so quickly. I never really thought about retirement as such.'

Dorothy initially says that she continues to work because she does not want to 'vegetate' at home all day. She has a similarly brisk view about the excuses that younger employees make for not coming into work. 'Older people appear to be more reliable. We take younger people on, and within a couple of days they're off sick . . . I'm of the opinion that if I don't feel very well and don't want to come to work, I'm sure that if I come into work I'll feel a lot better than if I stayed at home.'

However, Dorothy is not simply trying to prove that she has backbone by extending her working life. She mentions in passing that she and her husband are bringing up their thirteen-year-old grandson, after the death of one of her children. It is her duty as a grandparent that will define the span of her career. 'I need to sort my grandchild out financially before I retire. So if things work out properly, I shall probably stop in five years' time, when he is eighteen and I'm seventy-two.'

While women form only a slightly higher proportion of older carers than men, many assume a greater caring burden because of their traditional domestic roles as housewives and mothers. Sally Greengross, director of the International Longevity Centre, says older women carers are further disadvantaged because the pension system does not recognise what they do as 'work': 'Women do very badly at the moment from a financial point of view, because our current pension system doesn't treat them as individuals and doesn't compensate for time out for child-rearing and then caring for older people, which is now even more prevalent than for children.'

Gaye Rees is one of many women over fifty who have been severely stretched by the pressure of caring for ailing and elderly family members while doing a full-time job. Now sixty, Gaye retired in October 2005 from Yell, the directories company, where she worked at the firm's Reading head office as a purchasing manager. She liked her job, but her last four years before reaching Yell's (then) retirement age of sixty were overshadowed by a series of domestic worries. First, Gaye had to care for her ageing mother, who eventually died. Then her late father's brother and sister, who shared the family home in Portsmouth, reached a point where they could no longer cope on their own. As their nearest surviving relative, Gaye had to deal with the crisis. 'I was going down to Portsmouth an awful lot and it was getting very difficult. I was working hard, I was very targeted with work, and then at the weekends I was having to go down to Portsmouth.'

In 2004, in the middle of this period, Gaye's husband Ray fell ill with serious heart problems which required a bypass operation. Ray made a full recovery, but Gaye says the experience brought both of them up with a jolt. They agreed that Ray, who is two years older than Gaye, would retire early from his civil service job at the same time that Gaye retired from Yell. Their idea was to have more time to enjoy their own company, as well as their four grown-up children and two grandchildren.

By the time Gaye left Yell she had got her aunt into a nursing home; several months later, she found sheltered accommodation for her uncle. A committed Christian, Gaye has no doubt that she had to look after their wellbeing. 'I suppose because of how I've been brought up and because of [my] Christian beliefs, I feel you should be looking after the family.'

Gaye says that in her last years at Yell, she felt she could cope with the extra pressure on the home front and still do her job properly.

She adds, though, that the stress focused her mind on the fact that she did not want to extend her career beyond sixty. Furthermore, Gaye can see why other people in her situation might have chosen to give up work prematurely.

I have met quite a few people who have had to make that decision to take early retirement because of family needs when they become a carer. And of course, you can claim a small benefit but it's nothing like what people might have earned . . . It does happen that people become a bit embittered because they didn't want to give up work.

*

As these case studies suggest, there is no one-size-fits-all solution that will ensure fairer treatment for older women who want – in both senses – rewarding later careers. The complexity of the forces that undermine their position in the labour market defies a quick policy fix. Yet while these disadvantages are still formidable, they are not as great as thirty years ago, when women such as Gaye, Janet and Jane were starting their careers. The question is how much further this slow, incremental improvement can continue if employers fail to adopt a more sympathetic attitude to the demands placed on all women who work.

From a policymaker's perspective, there are grounds for optimism. The employment participation rate for women is at an all-time high, not just in Britain, but in many OECD countries (see Figure 6.2). This rate is bound to increase further in most advanced economies over the next few decades, due to projected increases in the state pension age for women. In Britain, as in other EU countries, it is also arguable that recent and imminent labour market

Figure 6.2: Labour force participation of women aged 50–64, 1970–2004

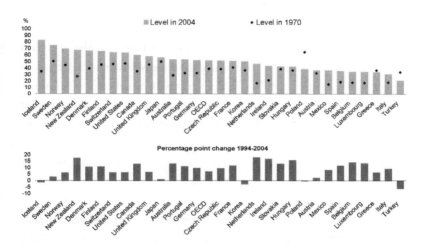

The data for 1970 refer to: 1975 for Iceland; Czechoslovakia for both the Czech Republic and Slovakia; and West Germany only for Germany. Source: Fig. 2.2. in *Ageing and Employment Policies: Live Longer, Work Longer*, p. 30, © OECD 2006.

and pension reforms will remove many of the inequities in the treatment of women which have restricted their retirement provision. Lord Turner, head of the Pension Commission, suggests that the burden of disadvantage carried by older women through their working lives will gradually lift as the next generation of women are placed on a substantially equal pension footing: 'I think those long-term problems from a previous labour market and from the lower NI contribution [for women] really only affect people who are already retired or who are five years away from retirement, rather than the bulk of the female employment workforce.'

The government agrees with Turner. In May 2006, it published a White Paper on pension reform in response to the Pension Commission's recommendations, with a view to setting legislation before Parliament in 2007. If the proposals outlined in the White Paper are adopted, the government predicts that the proportion of women entitled to a full basic state pension at sixty will rise from 30 per cent to 70 per cent between 2005 and 2010 (see Box 6.3).[*] The White Paper also acknowledges the economic contribution of carers such as Gaye Rees by proposing that 'anyone who has been in employment or caring throughout their working life could receive £135 a week at retirement in state pensions – which is £20 a week above the guaranteed income level'.[†] Meanwhile, in September 2006 the Department for Communities and Local Government published an 'action plan' for closing the workplace gender gap, following the recommendations of a commission headed by Baroness Prosser.[‡] The plan was targeted at women of all ages, but contained some measures of particular relevance to older women. They include better-funded training packages for those returning to work and an extension of the right to request flexible working to employees caring for adults.[§]

---

[*]Department for Work and Pensions, *Security in Retirement: Towards a New Pension System* (Cm 6841, 2006), p. 20.
[†]Ibid.
[‡]Women and Work Commission, *Shaping a Fairer Future*.
[§]*Government Action Plan. Implementing the Women & Work Commission's Recommendations* (Department for Communities and Local Government, 2006).

Box 6.3: Linda Walcott – why worry about the future?

The issue of pension reform is of no concern to many people, simply because they refuse to worry about how they will cope in old age. Linda Walcott, a 53-year-old nursery manager in Reading, is firmly in this camp.

Originally from Barbados, Linda is divorced with two grown-up daughters. She has worked for a public sector day nursery since she was thirty-eight, and vaguely remembers several financial consultants visiting the nursery in 1999, when the government launched its stakeholder pension scheme. Their advice confused her. 'With the older generation, they said there was no way we could afford to pay enough money into a pension to gain anything. There were also two other financial advisers who said when you get past fifty, you really need to be paying into benefits.'

Linda chose not to start a stakeholder pension. She will not be destitute in old age, because she has kept up her national insurance contributions. In 2011, she will have paid off her mortgage on her small house in west Reading. But when Linda retires, she will have considerably less to live on than her present, modest income. This prospect does not bother her. She swipes away the question about her future with a dismissive wave of her hand. 'What's the point in worrying? I mean, what is the point in worrying? You could sit here all day and say in ten years' time I'm going to need this, and you don't make it to that ten years. So you've spent this last ten years worrying about ten years that are never going to happen anyway. I'm not frivolous, but I think I'm here now.'

Such reforms, along with the more sweeping changes to the pension system envisaged by the White Paper, will help older working women in the long term. Yet there is a limit to how far changes in policy alone can alter the employment prospects of older women without a transformation of Britain's prevailing business culture. This point is underlined by Britain's feeble progress in closing the pay gap between older women and older men (a major reason for Prosser's commission). Between 1998 and 2004, the median average pay gap between men and women over fifty working more than thirty hours per week fell from just under 20 per cent to 17 per cent.* Alarmingly, these figures represented a slowing in the long term downward trend. Worse, the statistics for 2003–4 (the most recent year for which data are available) show a slight widening of the gender pay gap in this age group.

How could New Labour have had so little impact on the core problem, given the blizzard of policy initiatives and reforms it has unleashed since 1997 to help all working women, including those approaching the state pension age? The answer does not lie in Whitehall but in the boardrooms of corporate Britain.

Countless prejudiced employers undervalue older women because what they see is a human resources headache. From their perspective, women over fifty are likely to be underqualified, overextended at home, and out of touch with changes in the workplace. Jean Charmak, director of Forest, the Reading recruitment agency, confirms that such attitudes are a recurring problem for older women whom she tries to place in secretarial and administrative jobs:

If you're a PA who started at thirty and you've been with someone for twenty years, he [the boss] never thinks of you as fifty, because

*Annual Survey of Hours and Earnings 2004, in DTI factsheet *The Gender Pay Gap in Great Britain*.

you've grown old together. But it's much harder in this respect if you want to go in as a PA, and you've been out of work for twenty years.

Charmak suggests that women over fifty going back to work must be adaptable and willing to learn quickly. Stephen McNair, director of the Centre for Research into the Older Workforce, says many women in this age group are actually better in this respect than their male contemporaries:

Most men of sixty grew up in a world where the assumption was full-time employment for forty years . . . Because women [of the same generation] have been in a poor labour market position, and experienced breaks and part-time work . . . they're more used to finding themselves in places they hadn't quite planned for and making the best of it.

Unfortunately, flexibility can also mean vulnerability at the lowest-paid end of the labour market. Sarah Vickerstaff, Professor of Work and Employment at the University of Kent, argues that many older women are conditioned to accept pay and conditions that their husbands would probably not tolerate:

You could say [older] women are more flexible, in the sense that they're more manageable, malleable and biddable. Women will be more likely to take a lousy job with a poor salary because of the flexible hours, which fits in with looking after their elderly relatives or their grandkids. So it's not a wholly positive attribute. Women will put up with more in the labour market.

Sally Greengross and other campaigners for older people predict that employers will themselves have to become more flexible about accommodating the needs of employees over fifty as the labour force steadily ages. It is an alluring prospect for older women, given the additional domestic pressures that many of them face. Yet such a future is far from certain. There are too many imponderables, from the impact of globalisation on the labour supply to the proven ability of employers to minimise the impact of discrimination law on their business models. Even if the optimists in the age lobby are proved right, this future will arrive too late to help most women over fifty in today's labour market. The past has ensured that they are cast as losers in Britain's late shift.

7 Fantasy Island: the dream world of public sector pensions

The people who look like late shift winners in the short term are Britain's 5.8 million public sector employees.* On the one hand, New Labour's professed desire to take a lead in encouraging people to work longer means that there has never been a better time for older public sector employees who want to extend their careers beyond their traditional retirement age of sixty. On the other hand, most of them have retained the right to retire at or near sixty on an index-linked final-salary pension, following separate deals in 2005 and 2006 at central and local government level with the big public sector unions.

For Britain's 23.1 million private sector employees† – who are being exhorted by the government to work beyond sixty – this pension apartheid seems both unfair and unsustainable. They are right. Outside Whitehall and the TUC, there is universal consensus among independent experts that public sector employees are living on borrowed time in expecting taxpayers to fund their right to retire before the majority of the population.

---

* Labour Market Survey. Figures are for the three months to June 2006.
† Ibid.

Lord Turner condemns the government's climbdown in October 2005, when it reneged on an electoral promise and struck a deal with the public sector unions to retain a default final-salary pension age of sixty. The deal covered current members of the civil service, health and education pension schemes: 'It is not sustainable in the long term that we have this mismatch [between the public and the private sectors] and I think the chances that the deal which was done in October 2005 will stick are very low indeed.' Turner argues that taxpayers will not tolerate having to subsidise generous public sector pensions at sixty when the government – following his recommendations – is proposing to raise the state pension age gradually for both men and women to sixty-six after 2024 and sixty-eight after 2044.

We're having an intense debate on the state pension that 100 per cent of citizens get, as to whether as a society we can have a coherent system which might imply going from [a system costing] 6.2 per cent to, say, 7.5 per cent of GDP . . . This was the whole debate with the Treasury about affordability, and the Treasury arguing that it is not affordable . . . Switch over to the public sector side, and the figures say that even after the [government's] reforms, unfunded public sector pensions will go from 1.5 per cent to 2.2 per cent of GDP.

Turner believes that the proportion of GDP spent on public sector pensions could rise to 2.5 per cent of GDP, based on the latest official actuarial forecasts.

So there is a big debate about whether we can find 1.3 per cent [of GDP] for 100 per cent of the population, while on the other hand, we just say, 'Oh well, this is unavoidable, people [in the public sector] are growing old, so this is going to go from 1.5 per cent to 2.5 per cent for the 17 per cent of the population who are public sector employees.' I just don't think that will be seen as fair.

The government insists this arithmetic is wrong. At the time of the deal, Alan Johnson, then Work and Pensions Secretary, said that the agreement would achieve most of the projected cost savings that the government hoped to obtain from reforming the civil service, health and education schemes. Johnson based his claim on two grounds: first, people joining the schemes will have a pension age of sixty-five; and second, many existing members are expected to retire early by choice, thus accelerating the changeover to the new regime (see Box 7.1).

Johnson skated over the fact that the additional cost of supporting existing members who retire at sixty will still be immense. Turner says that in any case, the government is asking for legal trouble by running a two-tier public pension system:

I think I can see equal-opportunity-for-equal-work employment law cases staring us in the face here . . . And whether or not it can work in law, I think in justice, in ethics, it's atrocious. The beneficiaries of this [two-tier system] are going to be the high-income people who stay all the way, and the non-beneficiaries are going to be ancillary workers in, for example, the NHS – primarily women – who churn in and churn out . . . From a trade union point of view, the people who'll be on the new system will be the low income earners, and [especially] women, and the people on the old system will be the future permanent secretaries. I just think it's an absolutely bizarre deal in every single dimension.

Box 7.1: Robert – the reluctant early leaver

One group of former public sector workers are unwilling additions to the ranks of those leaving government service before they are sixty. Many older people in low-grade clerical and administrative roles lost their jobs as a result of continuing efforts to reduce the size of the central and local government workforce – often by subcontracting traditional civil service functions to private firms.

In 2005, at the age of fifty-five, Robert was made redundant by the Department for Environment, Food and Rural Affairs (DEFRA), when his job in Reading processing farming subsidies was outsourced to a private contractor. He has been unemployed ever since, despite applying for dozens of clerical jobs in the private sector. 'I do find that I have problems actually trying to sell myself. I probably don't make the most of the opportunities when I do get invited for interview . . . I usually go in feeling confident and relaxed, but I probably don't get my skills and knowledge across in a way that makes employers think, "I want this person for this job."'

Robert's other problem is a lack of advanced IT skills, which are required for many of the office jobs he targets. He is halfway through an Open University IT degree, but has had to stop because of eye problems.

Mild-mannered and diffident, Robert fears that he may never work again. His chief solace is his strong Catholic faith. He attends Mass several times a week at the local church that is linked to the school where his wife works as a teaching assistant (they have two grown-up sons). Robert is demoralised, but he recognises that as an ex-civil servant he is in a much better financial situation than many older unemployed people. He has a generous severance package from DEFRA, and when he is sixty, he will receive an index-linked civil service pension based on thirteen years' service and a final salary of £25,000 a year. At the same time, he will get a second final-salary pension from an earlier nineteen-year career with BT that began when the telecoms company was in the public sector. 'Financially, I'm probably better off than some people who are hunting for jobs, because I've got some money coming in.'

The government has taken a marginally more robust approach with the public sector unions over reforming the separate local government pension scheme (LGPS). In April 2006, the government issued new regulations covering the LGPS in England and Wales which took effect from October 2006.* These rules abolish the so-called 'rule of 85', under which members can retire on a full final-salary pension before the scheme's official retirement age of sixty-five, provided their total years of 'qualifying service' plus their age add up to eighty-five or more. According to the government, the rule of 85 breached the new age law by discriminating against employees who did not qualify.

Yet this reform is more limited than the government implies. It is still possible for existing members to retire early under the rule of 85 until April 2013, under a get-out clause called 'transitional protection'. Many long-standing local government employees will thus continue to retire at about sixty (or even younger in a minority of cases) on final-salary pensions, during a period when central government is trying to encourage the wider public to work longer.

Britain's heavily unionised public sector employees believe strongly in their right to keep these gold-plated pension perks at both central and local government level. The main public sector unions hailed the deal struck in October 2005 over civil service, health and education pensions as a victory for social justice. Six months later, the same unions claimed that over a million council workers joined a one-day national strike to protest against the

*Local Government Pensions Committee Circular No. 184 (April 2006), *Changes to the LGPS in England and Wales.*

ending of the LGPS rule of 85.* The unions argue that abolishing the rule will victimise the poorest local government employees, many of whom are women. For example, Unison – the biggest public sector union – says that almost three-quarters of contributors to the LGPS are women, who on average receive a pension income from the scheme of just £31 per week when they retire.

Meanwhile, many local government workers on much higher salaries feel their pension privileges are justified because they earn less than their counterparts in the private sector. Such is the unapologetic view of one employee in Reading Borough Council's environmental services department with a basic annual salary of £21,500: 'Everybody can find something to whinge about. I chose to go into the public sector, so as regards my pension, that's what I am entitled to.'

Regardless of whether these arguments have any merit, the government has compromised its ability to lead the debate on how the country adapts to the late shift by caving in to the unions on the public sector retirement age. Alan Pickering of Watson Wyatt, who was previously a senior official at the Electrical, Electronic, Telecommunications and Plumbers Union (now part of Amicus), says the government's retreat on the public sector pension age has thrown away an opportunity to set an example for the private sector to follow:

> They [the government] simply gave in to the trades union movement in a way that handed out all the wrong signals. If anybody could give a lead in terms of helping older workers fulfil their potential, it is the public sector . . . Because they are a big employer they ought to be

*The Local Government Association estimated that 400,000 employees joined the strike.

able to retrain and refocus people in late career. They've got the HR infrastructure to help people plan in later life, in a way that small and medium-size enterprises don't.

Belatedly, the government has recognised its misjudgement over public sector pension reform, at least on the narrow issue of affordability. In June 2006, a leaked memorandum by Hilary Armstrong, the minister in charge of the Cabinet Office, argued that civil servants should make a far bigger future contribution to their pension scheme. According to the *Sunday Times*, Armstrong said that civil servants must 'face the realities' of the rising cost of their pensions. She proposed that future contributions by the government, which in 2006 averaged about 19.5 per cent of salaries, should be capped at 20 per cent.*

Such realism is unlikely to spread to most central and local government workers in the short term. Instead, most of them appear to be in denial about the general taxpayer's continuing willingness to subsidise their privileged pension system. It is as if the public sector payroll has been magically insulated from the demographic trends that affect the rest of the country.

*

Reading's public sector breathes this early-retirement culture. In 2004 (the most recent year for which figures are available), there were 21,288 people employed in Reading in public administration, education and health, representing 21.7 per cent of the total number of local people in work.† As in the rest of Britain, Reading's public

---

* *Sunday Times*, 25 June 2006.
† *Labour Market Profile: Reading* (Durham: Nomis, 2005).

sector workforce is highly concentrated. The town's three largest employers are the borough council, which had 4,085 full-time and part-time employees at the end of 2004; the University of Reading, with 4,058 academic and non-academic staff in February 2006; and the Royal Berkshire and Battle Hospitals Trust, with 3,600 full-time medical and non-medical personnel in June 2006.*

Danny Downes, a 54-year-old driver for Reading Buses, a wholly owned subsidiary of the council, enthusiastically supports the right to retire early both from a personal point of view and in his official capacity as the local convenor for the Transport and General Workers' Union (TGWU). A convivial former soldier, Danny joined Reading Buses in 1985 and aims to retire at sixty-one, when he can claim his full final salary pension under the 'rule of 85'. 'I've seen too many people who've said, 'I'm retiring at sixty,' and then died at fifty-nine. I don't intend to do that.'

From the TGWU's cluttered office at Reading Buses, Danny is keeping a wary eye on the government's tentative efforts to abolish the 'rule of 85'. He is candid about what he sees as some of the age issues at the depot, next door to a former slaughterhouse. Danny says that it is a challenge training older recruits to drive the buses, despite the fact that they usually have plenty of driving experience:

> That isn't something that would help you get a job, just because you are older, because unless you've already got a PCV [passenger-carrying vehicle] licence, you're going to have to be trained. So therefore an older person is harder to train than a younger person, because it takes that much longer to sink in.

---

*Respective figures provided by Reading Borough Council and obtained from the university and hospital websites.

Mick Pollek, the TGWU's regional convenor at the union's main Reading office, does not share Danny's view about the slow-wittedness of some older people. Pollek looks and acts the part of a typical union man, with a shaggy beard, a blue TGWU sweatshirt, and an encyclopaedic knowledge of the fraught internal politics of Reading's local Labour Party. He also has a sharp mind, and sees both sides of the argument on age issues.

> There is a place for every age of individual in work. You shouldn't be put on the scrapheap because you're fifty-two, and that's it, and not get a job, because there's a wealth of experience there . . . [But] the days of being tied to your desk or your mill and having to bang on and on and produce should be long gone.

This is the bottom line for Pollek and millions of other trade unionists who oppose the government's plan to raise the state pension age gradually.

> If they're doing a job like you or me, why not? But if they're driving a dustcart, cleaning the streets or digging holes in the ground, then, yes, I am opposed to raising the age. Although people are living longer, [they] tend to be those who are not in such high-risk, dangerous jobs, or have not been brought up on beefburgers and pints of beer and are overweight like me.

Pollek thinks that the 'age-friendly' flexible career models of the future that are envisaged by age campaigners have little relevance to his members. 'It's no good saying to our binmen that you can take some time out to go and do some meaningful whatever, because we're looking at bins needing to be emptied.' His anger is reserved for what he sees as the government's attempt to cheat public sector workers out of their pensions inheritance. He says that until now, the chance to retire early on a final-salary pension was compensation for the relatively low pay of most employees in the public sector. 'Now to say, is it [public sector privileges] sustainable? Well, yes, it is, because it should be sustainable, and therefore government, whether it be through indirect taxation or whichever way it wants to, should maintain it and keep it to the levels that it ought to be.'

Anne Burton, Reading Borough Council's head of human resources, agrees with Pollek that the rates of pay for public sector workers have historically been low, compared with equivalent positions in the private sector. Yet she is convinced that the 'rule of 85' and other public sector pension perks cannot survive in the long term. In her view, the council has to encourage more older employees to extend their careers, for both financial and cultural reasons.

Burton works for a council that is generally regarded as one of the best run in south-east England. Nonetheless, she says that until recently, the council's approach to employing older people was not especially sympathetic. 'Part of the rationale for the council's expectation in the past that people should retire when they reached the retirement age [of sixty-five] was to ensure that there was employment for younger people who were looking to support families.'

Those days are over. The council now removes the names and ages of candidates on shortlists for jobs. It also checks regularly for any evidence of age discrimination among its workforce. And in principle, the council is happy to let full-time and part-time employees carry on working past the default retirement age of sixty-five.

The council's age-friendly message has registered with even the most obdurate members of its 4,000-strong workforce. In a windswept compound on a Reading trading estate, the borough's diminishing band of electricians – identifiable by their distinctive purple municipal vans – have plenty of complaints about the council. Their main gripe is the introduction of market testing, which forces them to compete for public sector contracts against the private sector. The electricians accuse the council of using market testing as an excuse for savage downsizing. But Jack, a diehard 58-year-old union man, demurs when asked whether older people are less likely to be hired and more prone to be fired by the council: 'I don't honestly believe that they would look at a younger person and an older person and say, "Well, we won't have this person because they're old." Because we do have an age discrimination agreement, so they really wouldn't be able to get away with that.'

The problem for Burton and other supporters of the new approach is that so far, the council's reforms have had no discernible impact on the age profile of the workforce, which remains heavily weighted towards people younger than fifty. In December 2004, 73 per cent of the total workforce were below the age of fifty, 25 per cent were in the 50–64 age group, and only 2 per cent were sixty-five or older. As Burton points out, there were substantial variations in the figures between the council's five main departments, known as 'directorates'. For instance, 82 per cent of 1,291 employees in the arts and leisure directorate were younger than fifty, owing to the relatively large numbers of younger people employed for sports activities. By contrast, 7 per cent of the environment directorate's 564 employees were older than sixty-five. Many of these staff were older women doing part-time cleaning jobs to supplement their pensions. Yet the overall picture is clear. While the council is striving to break down an entrenched early retirement culture, many of its employees are resisting.

Back on the trading estate, Jack the electrician expresses

considerable frustration that he is still working at fifty-eight. 'I always wanted to retire at fifty, because I think the retirement age of sixty-five or even seventy, like the government is planning now – well, you've got no time to enjoy your retirement.'

The paradox of the public sector's early-retirement culture is that it creates skills shortages which increase opportunities for older people who want to carry on working. At the Royal Berkshire Hospital, Jane Watts (see Chapter 6) is one of many older nurses who are highly valued because too many of their colleagues leave the profession early. Another is Aileen Blackley, a senior sister at the hospital, who will retire on her sixty-fifth birthday. Two months before this event, Aileen has no second thoughts:

> Of course I will miss the people but generally I won't miss the [hospital] trust. There has been huge upheaval. Change is not a problem; I've had a lot of change throughout my career. But the caring seems to have gone, and that bothers me. From my perspective it's very focused on the finances, and that's quite difficult . . . I feel very young, and I still feel I've got years ahead of me to do something, but I think it's time to do something else.

In October 2006, just after turning sixty-five, Aileen still had not decided what 'second career' she would follow in retirement. But there is a good chance that she will stay in the public sector, where there is a growing demand for pensioners like her with a high level of skills and experience. At the opposite extreme, the public sector is also a haven for older people (frequently women) who are willing to do low-paid, unskilled, part-time jobs such as cleaning.

The University of Reading, the town's third major public sector employer, illustrates both trends, according to John Brady, the director of personnel. 'Frankly, there are many areas of the university which would not be able to operate effectively if they didn't have a relationship with retired and over-retirement age members of staff.' Brady has in mind everyone from cleaners such as Jan Duffy (see Chapter 6) to emeritus professors (see Box 7.2).

Between these two extremes, Ken Beard, a 69-year-old part-time IT support assistant in the geography department, is a good example of the kind of skilled retired technician who is gold-dust to educational institutions. Indeed, he is ludicrously overqualified for his role. Raised in Reading, Ken spent more than thirty years as a senior maintenance technician with a local division of Burroughs, the American adding machine company. By the mid-1980s, when Burroughs had merged with Sperry to become Unisys, Ken was leading a multinational team that installed and serviced huge corporate computer networks for clients 'from South America to Siberia'.

Box 7.2: Ian Mills – measuring out his years

Ian Mills, an Emeritus Professor of Chemistry and Fellow of the Royal Society, shares a cramped lower ground floor office in the university's chemistry department with Robin Walsh, another emeritus professor. Ian retired as a full-time professor in 1995, when he turned sixty-five. While Robin takes a midday walk round the university's spacious grounds 'to check I can still do it', Ian explains over lunch in the senior common room how he has used his emeritus status to pursue a singular academic quest.

Ian heads an international committee of scientists whose task is to produce a global consensus on the exact weight of scientific units, many of whose original prototype weights have fluctuated over time. 'You may say it's an act of faith, but we believe all carbon atoms weigh exactly the same, and that they don't change as the years go by, and that they don't change throughout the universe. You see, we want definitions of the base units that are truly invariant, and are available to everyone, so that you don't have to go to a particular laboratory and get something out of a safe to realise what the definition is.'

Ian's life is not carefree, because his wife is unwell and needs a lot of help at home. But he is glad he has remained an active emeritus professor and is generally grateful for the university's generosity in giving him a berth in his old department. 'They wouldn't give me a laboratory, and I'll tell you what, they give me a room because I use it. I've seen quite a lot of colleagues retire and be given a room, and they don't use it, and within a year it's snaffled up and used for something else.'

True to his love of precision, Ian has set 2011 as the culmination of his retirement 'career', when he will present his committee's findings to the next-but-one international conference on weights and measures. Why not finish the committee's work in time for the next conference, which meets in 2007? 'We haven't yet persuaded all the important people that we have to persuade. And what we are suggesting is undoubtedly the way to do it, and we are shooting for 2011 . . . So I've got to keep going till 2011 and I've got to stand up before the conference, at which time I shall be eighty-one. But I'm hoping that I shall last out.'

In 1989, fed up with the constant travelling, Ken took voluntary early retirement from Unisys at the age of fifty-two. He ran a small IT services and support company with some friends for the next seven years, but the venture was not a success, and they eventually folded the business. Ken did not need to carry on working, because he had his retirement package from Unisys, his son and daughter had left home, and his wife still had a full-time job as an administrator at an international college in Reading. But he was bored at home, so since 1997 Ken has worked at the university (conveniently across the road) in a series of short-term, part-time IT support jobs. 'Being at home I'd be playing with computers anyway.

So I can learn a lot as well, getting paid a bit to look after computers. I'm keeping an edge by being in work – which is just a personal thing, really.'

There are also plenty of openings for retired people at Thames Valley University (TVU), a mile from Reading's more prestigious main university, provided they have relevant skills and experience. Nobby Clark, 67, took a job as a part-time driver at TVU a few months after retiring at the age of sixty-five as a manager in Reading for a building materials firm. Retirement did not suit him, especially as his wife still had a job. 'I was bored to tears, to be honest with you . . . Then I thought, "Well, I've got to do something. I can't just go down the pub every morning at ten o'clock and just stay there until she finishes work." So I looked in the paper and went for this job.'

Every weekday morning, Nobby delivers promotional material to schools, colleges and libraries on behalf of TVU. The hours suit him, as do the people he meets.

I've always been an early bird. Officially my hours are half past eight to half past twelve, but the college agreed I could do eight till twelve. I'm still in there at quarter past seven in the morning. I have a couple of cups of coffee, read the paper, and then I'm ready . . . What makes it nice is that I'm with nice people and they're very intelligent. And my customers who I go and see, like libraries and people like that, they're also intelligent. You don't get bad language, you don't get scruffy types, or arguments or anything else.

*

Reading's public sector, like the rest of Britain's local and central government payroll, is thus a place of contradictions. It combines an employer culture that is often more enlightened about older people than the private sector, with an employee culture that still clings unrealistically to what Lord Turner calls the 'golden age' package of early retirement and index-linked pensions. This package will inevitably unravel, because it is unjust and unaffordable. But the task has been made more difficult by the government's failure to dispel the public sector fantasy that the golden age has a future.

8   Signing on to the late shift

The research for this book began on a building site near Reading, with four craftsmen who were still working at an age when many of their colleagues had long since packed up their toolbags for the last time. It was suggested that the quartet were part of a labour market trend that could transform the workplace over the coming decades. Yet there is nothing inevitable about such a transformation. As the evidence from Reading shows, there is a gap between the wish of increasing numbers of people to extend their careers beyond the traditional retirement age, and the willingness of businesses to employ them.

The desire to carry on working is the sum of millions of individual choices. So, too, is the corresponding desire *not* to carry on working any longer than necessary. It is worth noting again that while this book has focused on people in the fifty-plus age group who wish to extend their careers, there are countless others who cannot wait to retire, or who have already taken early retirement.

What unites both categories is the fact that policy prescriptions frequently gloss over the degree to which individual motivation (or the lack of it) influences whether an older person stays in the labour market. Motivation is of course in part determined by the impact of wider social and economic forces. The decline of Reading's manufacturing base has demoralised a swathe of older blue-collar workers such as Clive and Patrick (see Chapters 2 and 5 respectively) Equally, the rise of Reading's IT economy has energised highly qualified older people such as Martin (see Chapter 4) to start their own businesses. The one constant in all these stories is the way – for better or worse – a person's character had a critical bearing on their later career prospects. Some, such as Dana Molecki, the PA who unexpectedly lost her job at the age of forty-seven (see Chapter 2), have the character and nerve to come back from adversity. Others, such as Maurice, the insurance broker (see Chapter 3), suffered a fatal loss of confidence at a critical moment in their professional life.

This individual diversity explains why there is no straightforward solution to the problem of how to accommodate the late shift, either in Britain or across the developed world. It is true that there are identifiable groups of late shifters, from people such as Joe Woodrow, the data analyst (see Chapter 4), who need the money, to those such as Mervyn Carter, the building site manager (see Chapter 5), who simply love working. Yet the circumstances that lead people to extend their working life in their sixties or older are far more varied, and in many cases more idiosyncratic, than the motives of school leavers and graduates entering the labour market.

It is no wonder that most of corporate Britain has so far resisted the idea of altering a trusted personnel planning model based on the assumption that the 'natural' age for retirement is somewhere between the current state pension ages of sixty for women and sixty-five for men. Older employees who want to carry on working past these standard departure points can easily look like trouble to a human resources manager. They may want to continue on exactly the same terms, like Del Wardle, the account executive at the printing firm Cox & Wyman (see Chapter 1). They may be looking to downsize to a part-time role in the same capacity, or move to a less demanding job. And they almost always have different timetables for when they will eventually retire, if they have any idea at all.

Faced with this human diversity, most businesses prefer to impose uniformity, in the shape of standard terms and conditions of employment and, above all, a default retirement age. Del was in a sense lucky; he persuaded his employers round to his point of view. Meanwhile, the new age discrimination law will at least force companies to raise the default age to sixty-five, with the prospect of this ceiling being eliminated in 2011, when the legislation is reviewed. Yet the law will not on its own eradicate ageism in the workplace, which takes many subtle forms, from passing over a well-qualified employee for promotion to screening out older candidates for job vacancies. The root of the problem is that much of the debate about how to find a solution begins from the wrong starting point.

Some age campaigners argue that because it is clearly in the interests of older people to extend their careers, and because the population is ageing, companies will eventually be obliged for business reasons to adapt their operating model to a greying labour market. As Sally Greengross says: 'We have to adapt jobs now to the sort of employees we will have, many of whom will be older . . . It's going to be a case of adapting to a new type of workforce, and we'll just have to change jobs so that people are not desperate to retire.'

Yet the evidence from Reading suggests that, retailers apart, most employers are reluctant to alter their operating model to accommodate older people. Legislation can force companies to treat the fifty-plus age group more fairly. What it cannot do is alter the fact that businesses exist to make profits, not act as welfare organisations. The best employers genuinely care for the wider wellbeing of their staff, but they care even more about the health of their balance sheet.

There is no inherent conflict between these two goals. In broad terms, a contented, motivated workforce is more likely to be productive than one which is not. Indeed, it is possible to sketch a benign scenario where companies eventually recognise that it pays to hire older people and then keep them happy, because they represent a growing proportion of the labour pool.

The difficulty with this vision is that it ignores the alternatives available to a company in the modern labour market. Older people will still have to prove their case to prospective employers, in a world of migrant workers, outsourcing to China and a permanent technology revolution.

It thus seems unlikely that demographic forces alone will make the future workplace a more welcoming environment for older people. And even if optimists in the age lobby are eventually proved correct, it will be a fairly distant future. The retirement of the baby boom generation between now and 2020 will actually reduce the proportion of people in the fifty-plus age group who are active in the labour market.

It is this generation – blessed with rising longevity and cursed with a creaking pension system – that urgently needs to break down age barriers in the workplace. Two factors in particular will determine its prospects: the impact of the law and the ability of older people to meet the demands of business.

Age discrimination law

In general, the treatment of older people in the workplace has failed to resonate with mainstream European politicians in the same way as earlier equal rights causes such as ethnic and gender discrimination. The United States passed its federal age discrimination law in 1967. But only two EU member states – Ireland and Spain – had comparable legislation before the European Commission directive in 2000 (see also Table 8.1).

Table 8.1: Age discrimination legislation in selected OECD countries

Country	Age discrimination legislation (ADL) and rules governing mandatory retirement (MR)
Australia	ADL at both federal (since 2004) and state levels. MR not generally permitted.
Austria	ADL since 2004. MR permitted once pension age of 65 for men and 60 for women is reached.
Belgium	ADL since 2004. MR not permitted in the private sector.
Canada	ADL at both federal and provincial levels. MR permitted in most provinces.
Czech Republic	ADL since 2001. MR permitted.
Denmark	ADL since 2004. MR permitted after 65, or earlier if objectively justified.
Finland	Age discrimination prohibited under constitution and the 2004 non-discrimination law. MR permitted in public sector.
France	ADL since 2001. MR permitted after 65, or earlier subject to certain conditions.
Germany	ADL since 2006. MR permitted after 65.
Ireland	ADL since 1998. MR permitted.
Italy	No specific ADL apart from protection against discrimination under constitution and labour law.
Japan	No ADL. Firms not permitted to set MR age lower than 60, rising to 65 in 2010.
Luxembourg	ADL since 2006.
Netherlands	ADL since 2004. MR permitted after 65, or earlier if objectively justified.
Norway	ADL since 2004. MR permitted in collective agreements.
South Korea	No ADL.
Spain	Age discrimination at work forbidden by 1978 constitution and Article 17 of the Workers' Statute. MR permitted after 65 under certain conditions.
Sweden	ADL since 2006. MR permitted after 67.
Switzerland	No ADL. Protection against age discrimination under constitution. MR permitted.
United Kingdom	ADL since 2006. MR permitted after 65.
United States	ADL at both federal (since1967) and state levels. MR not generally permitted.

Source: *Live Longer, Work Longer* (Paris: OECD, 2006), p. 105.

Since the directive, the most striking aspect of the process to introduce age legislation across the EU has been the general absence of political debate. In France – a particularly mute example – the relevant measures were passed in 2001 without any substantive discussion in the National Assembly. In Britain, there was considerably more public and political comment before the age law came into force in October 2006. But the event itself had none of the aura of a revolutionary moment that surrounded the first wave of discrimination laws on gender and race.

Britain's age law is not the product of a wellspring of popular outrage about discrimination against older people at work. Nor is it the act of a government that seems especially committed to the ideals that the law espouses, judging by New Labour's willingness to allow millions of public sector workers to continue to retire at sixty at the expense of the general taxpayer. Indeed, the law's uninspiring genesis makes it vulnerable to attacks by critics who claim – somewhat inaccurately – that it was imposed by Brussels. John Kay, the business commentator and academic, is not in this camp, but he nonetheless characterises the law as a futile piece of political meddling: 'The consequence of declaring non-discrimination a governing principle is to give power to regulatory bureaucrats and politically motivated obsessives, to create uncertainty in the ordinary conduct of business and to ask the courts to determine policies on grounds that have little regard to the costs and benefits of the alternatives.'*

There are also many sceptics who doubt that the law will make much practical difference to the treatment of older people in the workplace. They point to how age discrimination laws and related measures around the world have generally disappointed the original hopes of age lobbyists. In the United States, for instance, activists are 'convinced . . . that more legislation is needed' to update and improve the 1967 Age Discrimination in Employment Act.† In

*_Financial Times_, 3 October 2006.
† John Macnicol, 'The American Experience of Age Discrimination Legislation', paper for Economic and Social Research Centre research seminar, September 2005, p. 18.

2004, a survey of age legislation in several countries by Philip Taylor of the Cambridge Research Centre on Ageing concluded that much of this regulatory effort had 'not been particularly successful'.* Taylor cited the experience of Australia, where the abolition of mandatory retirement in all states by 1999 has prompted many employers to bypass the law and find 'other ways' to retire older workers. Overall, Taylor concluded that it was 'arguable' whether age legislation provided 'a suitable pathway for older workers and employers'.†

Against this background, it is worth stating an obvious point: Britain's law is already making a crucial difference to the workplace by denying companies the right to retire employees on age grounds before they are sixty-five. There are countless older people, such as Peter Dawson of Xansa (see Chapter 4), who have already benefited from the reform, and many more will do so in the years to come. In the meantime, Lord Turner is among those who argue that the reality of retaining staff till they are sixty-five will force employers to improve their treatment of all employees in the fifty-plus age group.

I wouldn't underestimate the extent to which legislative fact will change mindsets. I think once companies realise that they can't just get rid of people at sixty, and that if they try to do so they will have some nasty and expensive cases at 60–63, thoughtful employers will say, 'Wow, if I have to be willing to employ them all the way to sixty-five, I'd better start thinking back at employees aged 50–55 and looking at things like occupational health and retraining. Because what I want from this future 64-year-old is real productive work, if he or she has still got a right to hang around and be paid.'

* Philip Taylor, 'Age and Work: International Perspectives', *Social Policy and Society* (2004), vol. 3, no. 2, p. 169.
† Ibid.

The question remains whether the current default retirement age of sixty-five marks the furthest extent of the law's beneficial influence, or whether the government's promised review of the 65-year threshold in 2011 will result in its abolition. Across corporate Britain, there are plenty of companies that are uneasy about travelling any further (see Box 8.1). Nick Foster, director of human resources at Oracle's European head office in Reading, is typical of many HR executives in seeing endless legal problems if the default retirement age is abolished. He gives a hypothetical example:

You've got somebody who has worked for a company for forty-odd years. They're sixty-eight or sixty-nine, and they're starting to find it difficult to cope with the job as it is, and they are resistant to company-driven change, or they don't want to retire. If there is no legal right for the company to retire someone at some stage, there's a danger that we're almost encouraging both parties to end up in a tribunal and for a company to be forced to use all the incapability grounds to ease somebody into retirement, which is an appalling way to treat someone if they have had a successful forty-year career.

Box 8.1: The Pru's long and winding age journey

The experience of Prudential UK, the British division of the international insurance company, illustrates the resistance inside many large private sector employers to removing a default retirement age of sixty-five. In 2005, Prudential UK's human resources department launched what it branded an 'age journey', which was designed as an audit of the company's treatment of older employees ahead of the new age legislation. The HR team proposed raising the Pru's default retirement age in Britain from sixty to seventy. Such an eye-catching move, it was hoped, would establish the Pru in the public eye as a place that welcomed older people.

The proposal was put on hold in late 2005, when the company announced plans to buy out the minority shareholders of Egg, its majority-owned online bank. (Egg has since been bought by Citigroup.) The takeover involved a complex internal restructuring, and by July 2006 no decision on the new retirement age had been reached. Andrew Powles, Prudential UK's 'people policy manager', was visibly frustrated. 'I've done the engagement and the business is up for it. It's not helping the communications side, because people are beginning to ask, "What's the retirement age going to be?"'

A few weeks later, the senior management decided to adopt Egg's default retirement age of sixty-five for the whole of the restructured company. The company was thus compliant with the age law. But an opportunity had been lost to claim the high ground on mandatory retirement.

This position, however, is not universally shared by all British employers. The CBI's smaller rival, the Institute of Directors (IoD), says that about three-quarters of its members oppose the concept of forcible retirement on age grounds for company employees. In October 2005, the IoD expanded its views in an economic policy paper on pension reform written by its chief economist, Graeme Leach. He reiterated the IoD's proposal, submitted to the Pensions Commission, that the state pension age should rise to seventy by 2035, in order to make the system affordable.* Leach added that such a radical move (rejected by both the commission and the government in its 2006 White Paper) was not 'a silver bullet'. Employers, too, had a part to play:

Companies and other organisations will need to address the issue of managing an older workforce . . . Retirement is a relatively recent

---

* Graeme Leach, *IoD Road Map for Pension Reform: Creating a Pension System for the 21st Century* (London: Institute of Directors, 2005), p. 6.

idea. In the 19th century, most people worked until they dropped or could be provided for by their extended family. We certainly do not want to go back to the future, but the idea of retirement does need to be re-considered. We need to stop viewing retirement as a fixed point in the future. Instead, the concept of retirement needs to become more fluid.*

The hope of age campaigners is that by 2011 most private sector employers will come round to the IoD's view and accept that a default retirement age of sixty-five is actually an impediment to rational personnel planning. Sam Mercer, director of the Employers Forum on Age, says that the default age may even be a necessary evil to ease corporate Britain into a more flexible future:

A lot of employers were really nervous about how they were going to manage this retirement process [without a default retirement age]. They would have found a way to get rid of people. Our experience of working with employers is that you've got to let them see the light themselves. And by the time they have actually worked out that they would be forcing some of their most talented people to retire at sixty-five, it isn't a big issue.

Mercer – speaking on behalf of a corporate lobby group – thus echoes the view of age campaigners such as Sally Greengross, who believe that companies will eventually adjust their HR model to fit an older workforce. That in itself is encouraging. But if mandatory retirement is scrapped in 2011, it will not on its own herald a new age-friendly employment culture.

As Mercer acknowledges, employers who are determined to get

*Ibid., p. 45.

rid of older staff will probably continue to find ways to do so, like businesses in other countries where forcible retirement has been outlawed. In common with most age campaigners, she believes the law's cultural impact will be the equivalent of a slow burn, measured in decades rather than years:

> There are massive changes that we are going to have to make about how we work, when we take career breaks, and what sort of jobs we do at different points in our life. This is not going to happen overnight, or even in five years, just because the legislation is there. Come back in thirty years and let's see what the workplace looks like. Don't forget that on race and gender discrimination, we're talking about thirty years from there to now.

What the age law will never do is alter the terms of trade that define the labour market. Older people who want to carry on working will still have to prove that they are employable.

Meeting the demands of business

The case for employing older people is unanswerable, judged by the benefit to the economy. Alan Pickering of the human resources consultancy Watson Wyatt shares the view of almost every expert, including Lord Turner, that extending older people's working lives is essential for the nation's future prosperity. As Pickering points out, it is also critical to solving the pensions crisis:

> The work part of the equation is the key, as far as I'm concerned, [in the sense of] providing opportunities for older workers to stay in the labour market. It's good for older workers; it helps them to create more wealth for themselves. It's good for the economy,

149

because we need people to create wealth . . . and it also helps the pension system.

Pickering's analysis is supported by a growing body of economic research. In September 2005, Goldman Sachs projected that GDP growth in the world's six leading economies would be boosted over the next two decades if participation rates among older workers increased.* Goldman Sachs described a hypothetical scenario where participation rates for workers between the ages of fifty-five and sixty-four climbed gradually, so that by 2025 each five-year cohort was working at rates currently seen in the immediately preceding cohort. Thus, people aged 60–64 would be employed at the same level in 2025 as people between fifty-five and fifty-nine in 2005. Based on this projection, Goldman Sachs forecast that average annual GDP growth in Britain, France, Germany and Italy would rise by 2.2 per cent between 2005 and 2025, compared with a forecast rate of 1.5 per cent if labour participation rates remained the same. The equivalent differential in the United States was 2.8 per cent over 2.3 per cent, and in Japan 1.5 per cent over 1.2 per cent.[†]

In 2003, the economic consultancy Volterra Consulting conducted a similar modelling exercise in Britain for the charity Age Concern.[‡] The study, written by the economist Pamela Meadows, said that there were 430,000 people over fifty (with no upper age limit) who were not working and whose 'personal characteristics' were 'similar' to those of people in the same age group who were employed. Meadows calculated that employing the additional

* Sandra Lawson, Roopa Purushothaman and David Heacock, *60 is the New 55: How the G6 Can Mitigate the Burden of Ageing* (New York: Goldman Sachs, 2005).
† Ibid., p. 2.
‡ Pamela Meadows and Volterra Consulting, *The Economic Contribution of Older People* (London: Age Concern, 2004).

430,000 people would add around £12 billion to Britain's annual GDP. The report identified an additional 580,000 people in the fifty-plus age group who wanted to work, but did not possess these 'personal characteristics'. Meadows concluded that the total annual gain to Britain's GDP would be £17 billion, if both sets of older unemployed people found work.*

Unfortunately, most private sector employers do not think like economists. Their chief concern is increasing the company's profits, rather than adding to the sum of national GDP. And given their focus on making money, businesses often find what look like sound commercial reasons for *not* hiring, retaining or retraining people in their fifties or older.

Many of the fifty-plus jobseekers who do not share the 'personal characteristics' of those in work are close to unemployable in the modern economy. As Stephen McNair, director of the Centre for Research into the Older Workforce, says, 'there are people with low skills and very low chances of ever getting back into work'. Employers also cite the persistence of an early-retirement culture among many people in the fifty-plus age group – especially at the bottom end of the skills and income ladder – as a reason for not spending money on retraining them (see Chapter 5). Furthermore, older people are frequently seen as carrying additional baggage, whether in the form of health problems, extra caring responsibilities at home, or simply a basic inflexibility and lack of motivation. In Reading, the latter perception is encapsulated by the human resources director of a large British business services company: 'If you think about personal experience, I don't think anybody would deny that as one gets older one recognises in one's peers a probable increase in the mentality that says, "Been there, done that."'

*Ibid., p. 45.

Clearly such attitudes rest on dubious assumptions. There are also promising signs that more employers are starting to recognise the value of older people. Employment is rising sharply among people over fifty; in July 2006, the employment rate of men and women between fifty and their state pension ages rose 1.7 per cent on a year-to-year basis, more than quadruple the comparable rate for the entire working age population (16–64).*

The fact remains that finding and keeping a job is a marketing act on the part of the applicant. As the individual stories from Reading illustrate, employers are setting ever-higher standards for the quality of their workforce. There is a premium on skills and on the ability to upgrade them in a competitive environment. And above the most low-paid positions, anyone of any age who fails to pass both tests will rapidly lose their employability.

This reality is not as bleak as it sounds for older people. In Reading, as elsewhere, there are numerous capable and adaptable people over the age of fifty who have parlayed their experience and know-how into successful and rewarding later careers. Nonetheless, self-marketing is extremely tough for many in their fifties and sixties (or older) whose careers began in a more slow-moving economy, and who frequently encounter ageist prejudice when they apply for jobs. The challenge for them is to prove their worth, despite the prevailing corporate culture. Meanwhile, the political challenge is to do everything possible to strengthen the late career launching pad for older people who are serious about extending their working lives.

The government's efforts on this score should not be discounted, but its work is at best half done. Crucially, there needs to be far more investment in training and skills for older people. The government should also abolish the right of companies to retire employees at

*UK Labour Force Survey, Time Series Data, employment by age, May–July 2006.

sixty-five and bring forward the timetable for scrapping the public sector pension age of sixty, as a matter of social justice and political example. Such measures will not guarantee that all older people keep their footing in the labour market. But they will go a long way to ensuring that anyone over fifty who wants to work has a fair chance of success.

Winning the late shift

It will remain an unfair world, however, for those who need to extend their careers in order to achieve financial security in old age. For a start, a fortunate minority of their contemporaries do not have to compete at all. There are older public sector workers who continue to enjoy inequitable pension privileges. And then there are people such as Eddie West, a jaunty, retired vehicle fleet manager, who have played the corporate final salary pension game so well that they can realistically look forward to several decades of well-financed R&R.

Trained as an accountant, Eddie spent thirty-four years with the US automotive and engineering group Honeywell at its British head office in Bracknell, near Reading. He ended up as accounting services manager, responsible for all the UK subsidiary's financial processes, including vehicle fleet management.

Now being from a financial background, and being very much involved in payroll and that type of thing in the early days, I was very pension aware. I'm slightly unusual because I started paying AVCs [additional voluntary contributions] when I was twenty-six. So by the time I got to fifty-six I'd actually hit my maximum pension position in Honeywell.

In 1999, at the age of fifty-seven, Eddie took a voluntary severance package from Honeywell, which was about to be taken over by AlliedSignal, a rival U.S. multinational. 'It was two years before I had planned [to quit], but very nice the way I got it. I got a full package. I got some redundancy, I got a lump sum and I got a good pension. So I could afford to do it – that's the biggest thing.'

Eddie's worry-free life is far removed from the perpetual anxiety that envelops the ranks of low-skilled people in their fifties and sixties who have lost their jobs and are unlikely ever to work again. Some of them are familiar faces in Jobcentres across the country, scouring advertisement boards crammed with vacancies requiring skills that they have never possessed. Many others are less visible, having effectively dropped out of the labour market. It is almost impossible to quantify the number of older people who fall into this category, since they form an indeterminate mass that floats between different welfare pools, including incapacity benefit and the basic jobseeker's allowance. Yet it is clear that they will form a permanent, heavy burden on the public purse, as they drift towards an old age of penury.

Between these two extremes are those older people who want or need to work and have mastered the art of maintaining their competitive edge in the labour market. What qualities define them? The ability to moderate late career ambitions is one crucial attribute for people looking to downsize on the path to eventual retirement (see Box 8.2). Meanwhile, those who wish to remain in full-time employment have a harder road to travel.

Box 8.2: Tony Towner – downsizing with difficulty

At the age of fifty-five, Tony Towner took advantage of a voluntary redundancy programme and resigned from his job as a senior network engineer with BT. 'I was on a 24-hour call-out rota, which was the biggest bugbear, because I was getting disturbed left, right and centre. I could deal with most of the call-outs from home, so if I was woken at two o'clock in the morning, I would deal with it with a laptop and a phone. But my quality of life was going haywire.'

After thirty-nine years with BT, Tony walked away with a generous package. BT gave him three years' salary, with the first year's instalment net of any income tax. When he reaches sixty, Tony will receive a pension worth half his final salary, plus a lump sum worth one-and-a-half times that amount. This adds up to reasonable financial security for Tony and his wife, who works as a secretary, especially since their children have left home and the mortgage has been repaid on their neat bungalow in west Reading.

However, Tony was not planning to retire. He wanted to downsize to a completely different career. 'My big love is conservation, wildlife and the environment – that's my main hobby, really. So I was hoping to get a job in that field.' Tony realised his dream was too ambitious after several months of unsuccessful job-hunting for positions that would fit his hobby. 'There are plenty of vacancies, but they tend to go for people who've got university degrees or been to college . . . I didn't really look to see if there were opportunities out there. I just thought, "No, I'm going to leave BT and make a clean start with my life, and I'm going to do something totally different, and this is what I want to do."'

Tony revised his late career plan. At the end of 2005, nine months after leaving BT, he took a job as a caretaker at a private school near Reading. He earns much less than he did at the end of his career with BT, but Tony is far happier and less stressed. As a bonus, he may be able to pursue his interest in conservation work by helping the school with a nature project. 'The teachers want to start a wildlife garden, but it's a question of whether they can spend the money, and whether I'm willing to spend the time.'

The successful late shifters encountered in Reading are a strikingly diverse group. They range from Martin, the one-man web consultancy (see Chapter 4), through Brian Appleby, the fitted-kitchen entrepreneur (see Chapter 5) to Anne Murch, the petrol station manager (see Chapter 1). Two common attributes connect these seemingly unrelated people, just as they link others in their age group with rewarding later careers.

Firstly, they have all in different ways grasped the importance of matching their skills to the market. In this respect, it is irrelevant whether they sell web pages, kitchens or petrol; older people in full-time work usually have skills that employers or customers want to purchase. These late shifters also understand that their skills must be constantly adapted to keep pace with economic change.

Secondly, successful late shifters share a strong self-belief. It is the quality that has allowed Jane Watts to realise her childhood ambition to become a nurse (see Chapter 6); that has pushed Peter Wanless to keep applying for senior retail jobs, eventually with success (see Chapter 3); and that has kept Anne Murch's career on track, despite sudden bereavement and the loss of most of her savings.

It is easy to assume that their self-confidence is innate. After all, many others in their age group lose their late career bearings as a result of less serious professional and personal setbacks. The reality is more interesting. All these successful late shifters boosted their morale by gaining new skills at crucial points in their careers. In effect, their belief in themselves was reinforced by their willingness to engage with a rapidly changing workplace. They are the winners in an ageing society as Britain signs onto the late shift.

Epilogue

The people from Reading who feature in this book were all interviewed between May 2005 and May 2006. In the autumn of 2006, shortly before the book was completed, most of them were contacted again. This is what had happened to them in the meantime.*

Chapter 1

The four builders at Purley Magna went their separate ways at the end of 2005, when the luxury residential conversion was completed. Nine months later, three of the quartet were still working full time, with varying degrees of contentment.

Dave King (65, Workmates recruitment agency) has modified his dream of retiring with his wife, sister and brother-in-law to a new home in Australia. As planned, they went on an extended reconnaissance trip during the winter of 2005-6, and found their ideal spot near Adelaide. But they cannot afford the substantial bond

---

*A few people were impossible to trace. Human resources managers and other executives who gave interviews in a corporate capacity were omitted. The running order of interviewees is according to their order of appearance in the book. Their age in September 2006 and their place of work at the time of the original interview are noted in parentheses.

money which the Australian government demands from expatriates who settle in the country. Dave now thinks they may spend half the year in England and the rest of the year in Australia on tourist visas. Meanwhile, he is happy to carry on working, even though he does not need the income. 'I'm pretty fit, and while I've no real reason to continue full time, I do enjoy working.'

John Cochrane (63, Workmates) is also working full time, but with much less enthusiasm. Like many of his contemporaries, John is slogging on only because he feels he cannot afford to retire. 'I'm still fit enough to carry on, but it's the mental side that gets more and more difficult – the sheer boredom of it.'

John forgets about work by pursuing his interest in the classical world. His novel about ancient Rome is almost finished, and in his spare time he is also building two replicas of ancient Greek jury selection machines (known as *kleroteria*) for the University of Reading's classics department.

Brian Strange (65) appears to have realised his dream – shared by several other people in this book – of retiring to southern Spain, where he and his wife own a villa. He is still registered with Workmates, but has not been in contact with the agency for some time.

Dave Hicks (74, Workmates), the oldest of the quartet, also seems the keenest to extend his career indefinitely. His financial worries are now largely behind him, but Dave gets too much enjoyment from his job to contemplate retiring. 'I like work. I watch some of the people who have retired and they've either gone to heaven, or their topic of conversation is the prices at Asda or Sainsbury's.'

*

Del Wardle (65, Cox & Wyman) is happy to have won his battle with Cox & Wyman to continue working. He is also among the growing number of people who have benefited from changes to the rules in April 2006 which allow individuals to continue to work for the same employer while drawing a company pension. Del has taken his company pension, plus the lump sum that was due to him from Cox & Wyman, and put the money in a high interest savings account. The taxman will take some of this pension, but he will still be much better off than if he had retired.

Del has no idea how much longer he will stay at Cox & Wyman. 'The only thing that would stop me probably is the physical side of it. But once you've been doing the job this long, you know the job inside out. So stress-wise, it's not a problem.'

Ian and **Pat Reed** (59 and 58 respectively, unemployed) have abandoned their joint quest for jobs in Reading. In September 2006 they sold their house and moved to Helensburgh, near Glasgow, where their daughter lives. A few days before their move, Ian was apprehensive about their job prospects. 'It's a little bit daunting, but we'll have to see how it goes. Initially, we'll just grab anything that's going and take it from there.'

Anne Murch (70, Sainsbury's) continues to display the flexibility that has steered her through many unexpected career twists and turns. In the summer of 2006 she successfully applied for a job as an administrator in Sainsbury's back office at the Calcot branch, working 32 hours a week. 'I do like administrative work. It's back to where I started all those years ago in an office job with my dad.'

Anne is clear that money is her main reason for working, despite the pleasure she gets from seeing a job well done. She cannot see herself retiring for some time to come, given that she only has a small state pension. 'I'd like to say I can pack up, but I can't yet.'

Don (60, unemployed) is still struggling to overcome the negative mindset that afflicts many older people who have been made redundant. He has abandoned any thought of returning to his former career as a software developer, having been rejected for sixty-four vacancies. 'I suppose it's the old man's syndrome. I'm not going to get back into software.'

In August 2006, he began working in the bakery of a local supermarket, where his wife (who badgered him to apply) is also employed. Don is a bit dubious about his new job, and remains cynical about government efforts to help older people find work. 'You have all that rubbish on the TV about getting a job till you're seventy. What about *keeping* a job till you're seventy?'

Roy (57, unemployed) has finally lost his career footing, after years of drifting from one job to another in Reading's increasingly competitive labour market. He has failed to find a job since he was sacked by his last employer in the summer of 2005, despite applying for 'about 150' vacancies. Roy refuses to consider anything that pays less than £6 an hour, thus falling into the large category of older unskilled people who overestimate their earning power. 'There are some jobs out there that pay £4–£5 an hour, but they are lousy jobs for lousy pay. If you want a decent job, it's not there.'

Chapter 2

Pete Dunne (66, B&Q) found his enthusiasm for the 'social side' of work gradually wore away, and he left B&Q in November 2005. Now fully retired, he spends his time seeing his six grandchildren and pottering about in the garden with his wife. 'There were one or two little niggles at B&Q, but basically I'd just had enough. After working all that time, I deserve a little rest.'

Joan Mason (79, retired) continues to enjoy an active retirement, in common with many people of her generation. Joan remains a stalwart of the local Townswomen's Guild and goes on regular coach trips with other pensioners to shows and sights in London and south-east England.

Ray Buckland (59, Scottish Courage) has joined the ranks of those fortunate enough to retire early on a generous final-salary pension. He resigned from the Berkshire brewery in March 2006 and headed for the golf course. In September 2006 – following a brief return to the brewery on a short-term contract to train his successor – Ray began looking for a part-time job. He says the extra money would be welcome, although he is not complaining about his pension. 'It doesn't keep me in the lap of luxury, but I certainly wouldn't starve.'

Clive (59, unemployed) is still out of work and no nearer to acquiring the basic personal skills and computer proficiency that might land him a job. In the summer of 2006 he was interviewed for a store assistant's position at Sainsbury's Calcot store. He was rejected, but Clive was pleased that Sainsbury's at least bothered to write to him with the news. 'I felt quite uplifted by that. Things aren't so much of a void as they have been.'

Jim Thorpe (57, Gillette) and his wife continue to commute between their villa near Alicante and their home in Reading. Like many others who retired early on a final-salary pension, Jim's main concern is finding enough to keep himself busy and stimulated. 'The only thing I do miss about my old job is the problem-solving stuff. At work I was always dealing with problems, but my only problems now are things like DIY.'

So does he regret retiring? 'The way I looked at it, if I was going to retire, I'd stop working. So why stop working at Gillette and go and do something else, instead of retiring?'

Ian Little (58, Gillette) has found that his skills and experience are still in demand, despite the elimination of his job in the summer of 2005 as a maintenance coordinator. He decided to reapply for his former position in the tools department but was rejected, and left Gillette in October 2005 with a severance package that included a final-salary pension based on seventeen years' service. Ian got a job almost immediately with the Reading branch of Bailey Maintenance, a national building services company.

Looking back, Ian is surprised by how quickly he recovered from the shock of redundancy. 'Life deals you these blows, but you just have to get on with it. After about four or five weeks, it was like I'd never been there.'

Because his endowment policy has performed so badly, Ian expects to carry on working till he is sixty-five. 'I'd love to say I could stop, but you have to build up the pennies.'

Dana Molecki (57, Xafinity) is developing a second source of income as she approaches the state pension age. She remains happily employed as PA to the three top executives at Xafinity, the business software outsourcing company. If all goes well, she plans to continue working in her new job till she is sixty-five. 'I've got to be realistic. I'm getting on. At the moment it's great, and I want to stay there.' Meanwhile, Dana has branched into the buy-to-let business with her sister, in order to increase her eventual retirement pot. They have bought a small house in a former pit village near Newcastle, and are looking for other potential property investments.

Anthony (60) continues to demonstrate that regardless of age, the best defence against losing one's job in the volatile telecoms industry is having marketable skills. He has kept his senior technology role at the Reading offices of a large telecoms company, and is looking forward to retiring in a few years' time on a generous pension.

Chapter 3

Anne McCurry (71, John Lewis) is finally winding down towards her second retirement, after disliking the experience the first time. She has cut her hours slightly as a cashier at John Lewis's Reading store, and aims to retire in November 2007, when she will have completed twenty-five years with the company. 'What I want is recognition for twenty-five years' service, which goes on a big board in the store.'

Anne is less worried now about what she will do when she stops work. 'I'm a bit older now. I think I will be more settled.'

Jim Armstrong (76, Asda) has no plans to retire, despite hurting his knee in the summer of 2006 and taking several weeks' sick leave from his morning job as a greeter at Asda's superstore near Reading. He does not need the money, but, like many other pensioners in low-paid jobs, he wants a reason to get out of the house every day. 'My wife's still happy that I'm working there, which is the main thing. She'd rather shoot me first than let me retire.'

Mike Lancaster (66, House of Fraser) is still working full time in the lighting department of the retail group's Reading store in order to stave off post-retirement boredom. 'If I wasn't at work, I'd be staying at home reading, or going to the pub or a wine bar.' He thinks he may retire in October 2007, when he turns sixty-eight, but will see how he feels nearer the time.

Peter Johnson (57, Sainsbury's) is getting ready to join the retirement exodus to southern Spain, while continuing to work twenty hours a week as a health and safety office at Sainsbury's in Calcot. 'Some time in the next twelve to eighteen months' he and his wife plan to emigrate to a village near Cordoba in southern Spain, where their daughter, Spanish son-in-law and granddaughter live. Peter's wife still works as an administrator at the Atomic Weapons Establishment in Aldermaston. He calculates that their combined public sector final-salary pensions, plus their state pensions, should give them enough income to lead a low-key lifestyle. 'We're not going to be rich, but we can buy somewhere out there that's quite nice and still have enough for a rainy day.'

Peter Wanless (58) resigned from his job at the home furnishing chain Dunelm Mill's new Reading store after less than a year because of various management issues. In December 2006 he started a new job as an operations manager in the Reading area for Boots, the chemist. 'I am fairly confident that this is a job that will work out well for me, and it is a good company to work for.'

Peter is happy to be classed with others in his age group who cannot imagine a fulfilling life without work. 'I'm not sure what is the right retirement age in life, and I'm not sure that I'll ever retire. Whatever happens, I'll have to do something.'

Maurice (58, unemployed) sold his flat in the autumn of 2005 and rented a smaller one. He found the move so stressful that he stopped job-hunting for six months. Since the spring of 2006, he has only had two interviews for vacancies with insurance companies, both of which were unsuccessful.

Nonetheless, Maurice is lucky compared with many older long-term unemployed people. He reckons he will be 'okay' financially if he fails to get a job. He has the cash from the sale of his flat, a couple of endowment policies that will mature when he is sixty, plus a small pension he will receive at the same age from Norwich Union (which bought CGU, the descendant of his original firm, Commercial Union). And in the last resort, says Maurice, his family will look after him.

Chapter 4

Peter Dawson (62, Xansa) is one of many people in their early sixties who are grateful for the introduction of the new age discrimination law. Xansa's decision to raise its default retirement age from sixty-two to sixty-five brought the company into line with the legislation. Peter thus had three more years to build up a better pension fund. In October 2006 Peter's finances were further strengthened when he began to receive a pension from John Lewis, where he worked earlier in his career.

His only complaint is that having wanted to carry on working, he is currently a bit too busy. 'If money wasn't an option, I'd like to do less than I'm doing now. When I do retire, I think the shock will be all the greater.'

John (59, Cable & Wireless) has held onto his job as a data analyst, but is so disenchanted with work that he is prepared to undermine what already promises to be a fairly meagre pension fund. Financially, it would make sense for John to continue working at least until he is sixty-five. However, he is determined to quit when he is sixty-two, which is the minimum age for claiming his full company pension entitlement. 'I know the pension is going to be pretty rubbish, but I'm fed up with the job because it's so bloody boring.'

John's dislike of his job is combined with outrage at the poor performance of his private pension plan. He shares the widespread belief that many of the personal pension policies that were sold to people like him in the 1980s were based on fraudulent promises. 'I'm now putting more into my pension than I can ever see myself getting out. I'm putting in more money but my pension is going down.'

Terry (66, ING) has decided to carry on working part-time for a little longer before finally calling it a day. In September 2005, when he turned sixty-five, he was offered a new contract by ING Direct, with the option of moving to another department and possibly working longer hours. Terry decided to stay in his low-key morning job in the post room, thus leaving his afternoons free for 'luxury time'.

Joe Woodrow (65, Foster Wheeler) is still managing to keep his late career on track as a contract worker in the volatile technology sector. In the summer of 2006, he was rehired through his recruitment agency by Foster Wheeler to work as a database analyst on two large-scale engineering projects. Joe reckons this work will 'see me through to my seventieth birthday', his target date for retiring.

Martin (54) has discovered that his experience and long-term contacts are not enough to sustain his one-man web design and technical writing consultancy. Since 2005, some of the work he was getting from clients who knew him from his earlier career has dried up. 'The business tailed off slightly, so I'm having to spend a bit more time raking up new customers.'

Martin and his schoolteacher wife are still thinking of moving from Reading when he is about sixty, and their teenage son has left home. They would like to escape the Thames valley's notorious drizzle, possibly by settling on the south coast. 'In terms of my life plans the job helps, because I can do it anywhere.'

Chapter 5

John Daly (79, Workmates) has confronted the fact that his body is no longer equipped for demanding physical labour. In September 2006 he finished a building site job stacking plywood, with no other work in sight. His knees and hips are starting to play up, and John thinks it may be time to finish for good. 'It's just coming to the stage now where I feel I might be finishing. When you get to this age, nearly eighty years old, you go to the doctor and he says, "Your machinery is wearing out."'

Patrick (59, unemployed) remains locked in the mentality that ensures many older unskilled jobseekers will never work again. He insists he cannot afford to take one of the low-paid 'shelf stacker' jobs that exist in abundance in Reading, because he still has seven more years left on his mortgage. 'I have to get a job that pays me £200–£300 a week. Anything less than that, and I'd be out on the street. I said to the Jobcentre, "If I get a job at less than £200 a week, will you make up the rest?"'

Brian Appleby (74, self-employed) is still struggling to find carpenters for the small kitchen-fitting business that he started for his deaf son Ian. Brian does not need the money, but having retired once, he has no plans to repeat the experience. 'The business keeps me on the edge, I suppose. The idea of sitting back and just putting on a pair of slippers – oh my God, it would drive me crazy. I haven't got any slippers, by the way.'

Mervyn Carter (69, Daniel Owen) began a new contract in the autumn of 2006 as the site manager for a 'refurb' job on an upmarket housing estate near Reading. His skills and experience are in such demand that he can plan the last phase of his career as he pleases. 'The earliest date I can envisage I'm going to retire is when I'm seventy-two. That's when the wife [an auxiliary nurse] retires. But if I still feel as good as I do, I'll carry on.'

Chapter 6

Jan Duffy (69, University of Reading) is still one of many older women who do low paid, part-time work to supplement an inadequate state pension. She is not yet ready to retire, despite a recent wave of redundancies that has more than halved the number of cleaners at the university's Bulmershe campus. 'I decided that I'd stay on anyway, because I don't like hanging around the house. If I feel bad [physically], I'll have to jack it in.'

Jane Watts (60, Royal Berkshire Hospital) remains delighted that she was given an opportunity late in her career to pursue her ambition to be a nurse. 'I'm very happy in what I do. I'm learning all the time.' She is sticking to her target of retiring at sixty-five, provided she can cope physically with the work.

Joan Whyte (59, University of Reading) carries on happily as a secretary in the university's Italian department, working four days a week. She counts herself lucky that she enjoys her job, because she is convinced that her age would stand against her if she applied for another comparable position. Joan still aims to retire at sixty-five, but her later life plan extends no further. 'I have no idea what I'll do when I retire. I don't think about it.'

Janet Tabatabai (56, Thames Valley University) continues to work as a part-time receptionist. She is looking forward to starting her university degree at TVU in 2008, but in the meantime, enjoys the social side of coming into work every day.

> To be honest, I don't think I'd have many friends at home to visit nowadays. I think so many people [of her generation] do go out to work that if I was at home I'd be so lonely. With my colleagues, we don't actually socialise out of work, any of us, but we do have a good time when we're here.

Gaye Rees (61, Yell) maintains her balancing act between family concerns and her own retirement interests. Her aunt died in the summer of 2006, and Gaye continues to keep an eye on her uncle in Portsmouth. At the same time, she has begun to think seriously about what she might do as her main post-career occupation. Ideally, she would like a voluntary job where her computer and management skills were valued. 'I've got so many contacts with so many people, but I'm just trying to be a bit picky about what I do.'

Linda Walcott (54, Mary Seacole Day Nursery) dismisses the new age legislation and government plans to raise the state pension age as just more ruses by politicians to make everyone work longer. 'What the government's saying is that they want you to work till you die. What they don't want is for you to get a pension.'

Linda's own retirement plans remain unchanged. She expects to continue as the nursery's deputy manager until she is sixty, and then retire on whatever pension the state will give her.

Chapter 7

Robert (55, unemployed) is starting to suffer the kind of mental and physical attrition often associated with long-term unemployment. He has allowed his weight to creep up to 16 stone, and as a side-effect, his eyesight problems have worsened. 'I hope I'll work again, even if it's just for a few years. But I must confess that the longer I'm out of a job, the less likely I am to get one.'

Danny Downes (55, Reading Buses) still aims to retire early at sixty-one on a full final-salary pension, as a beneficiary of the government's decision to retain the 'rule of 85' for local government workers like himself who qualify before April 2013. As the senior TGWU official at the main Reading bus depot, Danny is mindful that not everyone is as fortunate as himself:

> Pensions is a hot topic at the moment. The majority of people [at Reading Buses] are concerned about how they're going to cope when they retire, and they see now, more and more, that pensioners are actually struggling. We have young people now actually thinking about their pension, rather than getting to forty and saying, 'I really should be in a pension.'

Aileen Blackley (65, Royal Berkshire Hospital) retired as a senior sister in July 2006. In October she went on a long family holiday to India, and then began tentatively thinking about a new post-retirement vocation. She says retirement is 'great'. To her surprise, she does not miss her previous high-pressure hospital job. 'I thought I would be bereft, but I'm not.'

Ian Mills (76, University of Reading) is pacing himself to keep going until he is eighty-one, when he aims to have completed the work of his international committee on scientific units. 'You want to go on using your brain, don't you . . . I mean, if I didn't have this activity and I were just to garden, or did a bit of sailing, which I like, I'd decay. My brain would decay.'

Ken Beard (69, University of Reading) is steadily moving towards full-time retirement. In August 2006, following a brief lay-off, he was rehired by the University of Reading's geography department on a six-month contract to do IT support for ten hours a week. Ken will continue for as long as he is wanted, but work is now an interlude between various projects at home. He is writing an autobiography in reverse chronological order, and is devising an irrigation system to water his flowers while he and his wife are on holiday. 'Whether I reach completion on these items or not doesn't really matter, as I enjoy the doing part.'

Nobby Clark (67, Thames Valley University) says 'everything's ticketyboo' with his job as a part-time van driver. He definitely will not retire before March 2007, when his mortgage will be paid off. Nobby says he may carry on for as long as his wife, now sixty, is happy for him to be working. 'I think sometimes you're making a mistake just retiring and not keeping ticking over. People say, "I'll work till sixty-five and then put my feet up." You might as well order your box early.'

Chapter 8

Eddie West (63, retired) is managing his gradual retirement with all the care he devoted to building up a sizeable pension pot. His main post-retirement activities have been acting as a part-time consultant for Yell, the business directories company, which wanted help with its extensive vehicle fleet; and setting up the Institute of Car Fleet Management, the industry's first professional body. Eddie retired from both jobs in 2006, and now only does occasional work as a security steward at Windsor racecourse, where he supervises the VIP enclosure. 'It really is fun, but it's certainly a retirement fallback job, because once I've paid the tax it's just pocket money.'

In Eddie's view, one of the secrets of a fulfilling retirement is to let go of what you had in your previous career.

In business, you have a lot of power. I'll give you an example. My spending power with the automotive industry [when he was in his full-time job at Honeywell] was £15 million per year. It gives you a lot of position, a lot of focus – you're the man. The day you walk away from it, that's it. You don't even exist. But you've got to be prepared to do that, and accept it.

Tony Towner (56, retired) is still happily employed as a school caretaker. He has no regrets about leaving his much better-paid job as a network support manager at BT, and downsizing to a more congenial workplace. 'In my last years at BT, it was getting harder and harder to get out of bed. The call-outs seemed to be increasing for one reason or another. Although there were aspects of my old job which I loved, it was the rota that did me in.'

Acknowledgements

The Joseph Rowntree Foundation awarded me a writing fellowship in April 2005 to undertake this book. I would like to thank the foundation and Richard Best, chief executive until December 2006, for this generous financial support. I am particularly grateful to Donald Hirsch, the foundation's special adviser, who provided valuable advice throughout the research and writing.

As is clear from the text, I have benefited greatly from the help of various experts on older people and the workplace. Among campaigners for older people's rights, I am indebted to Patrick Grattan, chief executive of The Age and Employment Network; Sam Mercer, director of the Employers Forum on Age; and Sally Greengross, chief executive of the International Longevity Centre in London and former director-general of Age Concern.

While this book is not an academic study, I am grateful to the following academics who kindly shared their research with me and provided an essential sounding board for testing my own conclusions: Stephen McNair, director of the Centre for Research into the Older Workforce; Philip Taylor, former director of the Cambridge Interdisciplinary Research Centre on Ageing and, since 2006, Professor of Ageing and Social Policy at Swinburne University of Technology, Australia; Sarah Vickerstaff, Professor of Work and Employment at the University of Kent; and Sue

Yeandle, Professor of Sociology at the University of Leeds.

I am grateful to Lord Turner for briefing me about the work of the Pension Commission and for sharing his views about pension reform. Alan Pickering of Watson Wyatt was equally generous with his time and expertise on the same subject.

In Reading, I wish to thank firstly more than 100 local people over the age of fifty who willingly agreed to be interviewed about their career and retirement plans. I am grateful to all of them. I owe particular thanks to Mike Coulson, Sue Culver and Carol Charles at the Reading Training Employment Advice Shop, who allowed me to attend a series of job clubs for the over-fifties and provided an indispensable ground-level insight into the challenges facing older people in today's labour market.

My agent, Jane Turnbull, gave essential support from the book's conception to its publication. As always, I am very grateful to her. I am equally grateful to Alan Gordon Walker at Politico's Publishing, who commissioned the book and offered expert editorial guidance during the research and writing.

My mother and stepfather, Angela and Humphry Crum Ewing, kindly gave me a base during my frequent visits to Reading, and shared their extensive knowledge of an eclectic range of local and national subjects, from the demolition of the town's old brewery to the funding of the Universities Superannuation Scheme. They were constantly hospitable and helpful.

My greatest debt is to my partner, Tess Poole, and our daughter Hannah, who have provided endless help and encouragement over the past year.

Index